Portuguese Cooking

Portuguese Cooking

The Authentic and Robust Cuisine of Portugal

Journal and Cookbook

Text and illustrations by

Carol Robertson

Photographs by
David Robertson

North Atlantic Books
Berkeley, California

Portuguese Cooking: The Authentic and Robust Cuisine of Portugal

Published by
North Atlantic Books
P.O. Box 12327
Berkeley, California 94701

Cover and book design by Paula Morrison
Typeset by Catherine Campaigne
Printed in the United States of America

Portuguese Cooking: The Authentic and Robust Cuisine of Portugal is sponsored by the Society for the Study of Native Arts and Sciences, a nonprofit educational corporation whose goals are to develop an educational and crosscultural perspective linking various scientific, social, and artistic fields; to nurture a holistic view of arts, sciences, humanities, and healing; and to publish and distribute literature on the relationship of mind, body, and nature.

Library of Congress Cataloging-in-Publication Data

Robertson, Carol, 1942–
    Portuguese cooking : the authentic and robust cuisine of Portugal : journal and cookbook / text and illustrations by Carol Robertson : photographs by David Robertson.
        p.   cm.
    Includes index.
    ISBN 1–55643–158–9
    1. Cookery, Portuguese.   2. Portugal—Description and travel.
I. Robertson, David,   1930–   .   II. Title.
TX723.5.P7R63   1993
641.59469—dc20   93–1684
                                                                        CIP

2   3   4   5   6   7   8   9   /   97   96   95   94

Acknowledgments

Many individuals have helped in large and small ways with this book, and their contributions are appreciated. A special thanks to Jennifer Robertson-Geary for her advice and patient typing, Erica Robertson for her fine suggestions and proofreading, Pat Geary who contributed Rosella Lopes's recipes, Esther Saldanha, a native of India, who generously contributed advice and authentic family recipes from Goa, Bob Kayser of Rochester Institute of Technology for photographic assistance, Anna Servati for her hard work on the final manuscript, Francis Lennie for the index, Marie Winkelstern for imparting her sense of careful cooking and good ingredients, Jim Geary who brought us hard-to-find ingredients from the Portuguese community in Stonington, Connecticut, and especially to the many nameless Portuguese people who showed us ingredients, methods, and measurements, helped us with recipe translations, and walked us through dozens of restaurant kitchens!

Table of Contents

Olive Appetizer / 74
Piri-piri 1 / 75
Piri-piri 2 / 76
Portuguese Corn Bread (Broa) / 77
Portuguese Country Bread / 78

Soups

Chicken Rice Soup with Lemon and Mint / 82
Potato and Kale Soup / 83
Tomato and Sausage Soup / 84
Tomato Açorda / 85
Shellfish Açorda / 86
Rosella's Fish Chowder / 88
Caldeirada (Portuguese Fish Soup) / 89

Vegetable and Salads

Braised Carrots / 92
Cauliflower with Piquant Sauce / 93
Broad Beans with Bacon and Sausage / 95
Peas Algarve Style / 96
Cold Egg Pie with Peas and Sausage / 97
Roast Potatoes with Olives / 99
Twice Cooked Potatoes / 100
Fragrant Rice / 101
Tomato and Mixed Greens Salad / 102
Mixed Pepper Salad / 103
Eggplant Salad / 104

Seafood

Marinated Mussels / 107
Cold Mixed Seafood Platter / 108
Grilled Trout / 110
Shrimp (Oyster) Curry / 111
Deep-Fried Squid in Batter / 113
Baked Red Snapper with Tomatoes / 115
Grilled Shrimp / 116
Shrimp with Sweet Red Peppers / 117
Bacalhau / 118
Bacalhau à Gomes de Sá / 119
Bacalhau Fritters / 120
Bacalhau with Chick Peas / 121
Bacalhau with Eggs / 122
Baked Bacalhau with Sausage / 123

Meat and Poultry

Liver and Sausage with Fried Potatoes / 126
Pork and Clams in a Cataplana / 127
Tripe Oporto Style / 129
Chicken (or Rabbit) Braised in Red Wine / 131
Braised Leg of Lamb with Sausage / 133
Jeera Meera Masala / 135
Cozida (Portuguese Boiled Dinner) / 137
Roast Chicken with Piri-piri / 138
Roast Pork with Piri-piri / 139
Roast Pork with Figs / 140
Roast Suckling Pig / 142

Desserts

Introduction

PORTUGAL IS A special place. We arrived for the first time by air into Lisbon, typical tourists, with no other ambitions than to see the sights. But the lure of the country and its people began to work its magic almost immediately.

A small country, only 150 by 350 miles, Portugal defends its corner of the Iberian peninsula against the larger influence of Spain. Everywhere are clues to its glory days when Prince Henry the Navigator and other brave explorers made Portugal the queen of the seas. That's another story.

We fell under the spell of a quiet, beautiful country, its dignified, kind and friendly people, and, of course, the food. It wouldn't be fair to say that the only reason we travel is to eat — but the cuisine of an area, the cooking "culture", so to speak, very much helps to define a people. Have they inhabited a poor country? Have they seen the sweep of foreign armies and occupation? What are the special indigenous herbs, spices, fruits, and vegetables? What is the geography? Is most of the land near the sea, on dry plateaus, in high mountains? Are the winters long and harsh, the summers wet or dry? Special festivals, religious beliefs—all these and more— provide subtle clues, and each leaves its trace, sometimes a faint leitmotif, sometimes a dominant melody, each providing part of the symphony that is a cuisine. Countless people through the centuries have taken the ingredients, the occasion, and the conditions, and with an instinctive assurance have created a body of recipes and dishes: a cuisine that is exactly appropriate. Mother Earth provides the balanced and nutritious raw materials; the people create the cuisine.

The sturdy Portuguese cuisine is highly flavored and complex, bringing together influences from Europe, Africa and the Muslim world. It relies heavily on pork and seafood of all kinds, as well as tomatoes, olives, kale, hot and sweet peppers, almonds and eggs, parsley, coriander, garlic and mint, spices such as nutmeg, cloves and cinnamon, and, of course, olive oil.

It is hard to know just where and when the idea came to us to write a journal with recipes. We have always kept very careful records of each day of a journey—long rambling descriptions—and as we reread them, we realized that nearly every page contained—alongside accounts of people, places, and events—detailed descriptions of what we ate— as well as menus and notes about ingredients, presentation, and ambiance. Some of our most appealing entries were collected while traveling in Portugal.

No effort is made at chronology. Each chapter stands by itself, describing a day or two, our experiences, and the food. Please travel with us through this lovely country, meet the people, see the sights through our photographs, and later use the recipes to recreate the delicious Portuguese cuisine.

Stories
of Portugal

Food from the Sea:
The Fishermen of Nazaré

AN EASY DRIVE north of Lisbon lies Nazaré, an ancient fishing village and twentieth century resort. We drove into town one afternoon and maneuvered our car downhill through the narrow and crowded streets toward the beach. Locating a room was not easy, as the town has already been discovered, but after several tries we found a clean, pleasant room, and as was our habit, rested a bit before venturing out to explore.

Our guide books told us that this was an unusual town, really comprised of two towns: one on the beach and one on a high cliff above it. Until very recently there was no harbor for the fishermen, and each day they had to launch their boats by rolling them over logs and into the pounding and dangerous surf. Tractors or teams of oxen hauled the returning boats onto the beach. Although a harbor has since been constructed for them, the families still congregate on the beach daily to watch for the returning boats.

Mid afternoon is a quiet time in Nazaré, but by five o'clock the second part of the day begins, and continues long into the evening. The streets were crowded with beachgoers and local families when we emerged from our hotel on this hot, sunny, late afternoon in July. We worked our way along the main avenue for a few streets to Praia (or beach), the name the locals give to their old town, or fishermen's quarter. Small whitewashed houses line the narrow alleys that bank steeply up from the beach. Turning into the first street we were quickly engulfed in family life. Each door stood open, and a chair or two was placed outside, sometimes with a tiny table. Children ran and shouted, playing with balls or carts, women finished hanging their wash across the alley, and men sat sipping red wine or mending nets. Most houses had set out small braziers, and a few pieces of wood and charcoal burned under grills.

We continued for some time strolling up one street and down another, always staying in the old quarter. The clothing worn by the adults contributed to an overwhelming sense of being transported into another era. The men wore dark plaid shirts and trousers, and many were wearing long black stocking hats said to keep the sea spray from their necks. All were barefoot—these are beach people—as were the women, who looked quite saucy in their short skirts and many petticoats that swished about their knees as they walked. We passed several front doors where the women had a few hand knit fishermen's sweaters to sell. Soft browns, grays and whites—the colors of the sheep and in only the most general sizes— they were quite beautiful in a rough way. We bought three.

After a bit the women began to grill whole sardines, and their delicious smell reminded us that it was time to find a restaurant. In the street somewhat behind the old quarter we found several cheery seafood establishments, all owners actively soliciting our business, trying to draw us to their five or ten outdoor tables with the promise of the freshest, cheapest, and most varied cold seafood platter. Choosing one, we were presented almost immediately with a basket of delicious, crusty Portuguese bread, a small dish of marinated olives, a bottle of the local white wine, and an enormous platter of an incredible variety of seafood. In its center rested a large dish of garlicky mayonnaise and many lemon wedges. We spent a delightful hour picking our way through crustaceans of many types, shrimp, deep-fried calimari rings, and pieces of grilled fish. Our smiles of enthusiasm must have showed: our waiter offered to take our picture!

Later that evening, strolling along the beach, we watched more men mending nets and women cutting open hundreds of small fish to dry on screens raised and tilted on stands pounded into the sand. At the other end of the beach there was what amounted to another town: the tents of the bathers—an extraordinary sight of perhaps one thousand pastel cabanas lined in precise rows on the sand, making a permanent summer installation. The sense of three towns coexisting side by side, somewhat oblivious to each other, was interesting. Tomorrow we would visit the third town, Sitio, built directly above Praia on the tallest cliff face in Portugal.

Our excursion the next morning was made easier by a ride on a funicular straight up the cliff. In a few minutes it transported us to yet another world. Here, the women wore long black dresses which, along with a black shawl that covered them from head to ground, made it difficult to see the person underneath. How perfect each town's clothing was: the short-skirted, barefoot beach people below and the shrouded women on the cliff outfitted to resist the constant strong winds of their high village.

The view was spectacular from this town, with the cabanas below on the near beach and the fishing boats and the nets in the distance. We walked the more crooked, sheltering streets of the upper town and ate a simple lunch of whole fresh grilled fish, tomato salad, and crusty Portuguese bread served to us by a housewife who turned the narrow street in front of her home into a two-table restaurant. At about noon she lit a small charcoal fire and was instantly in business. Delicious.

Later that day we returned to the lower town for a swim. The surf was incredibly rough, and we appreciated the arduous task of the fishermen of past generations who had to launch their small wooden boats directly into it. Nazaré has no natural harbor, and the nearby man-made one of recent years must have been a godsend. By late afternoon the fishermen's families were standing on the beach among the bathing tourists, craning their necks to catch a first glimpse of returning boats. We watched as wives gave scowling looks to their men if their eyes strayed from the horizon to the topless bathers at their feet. Although Americans seem to be a bit too shy to go topless, this beach was full of German, French, and Scandinavian women all eager for the perfect tan. What a conflict of cultures!

That evening we dined on that most typical of Portuguese dishes: potato and kale soup, traditionally served with corn bread, as well as succulent roast chicken with a fiery sauce called piri-piri, white wine, and a distinctly Portuguese version of flan flavored with port wine.

Later, falling asleep, we mused that we were certain we had found the quintessential quiet fishing village at Nazaré—until six o'clock the next morning. What appeared to be a closed warehouse the day before had been transformed overnight into a regional fish market. The noise was deafening. We were awake, and to make the best of it we took our camera, went downstairs and across into the market, and spent a happy couple of hours photographing brawny women wielding cleavers, while shouting their prices and the merits of their fish and hauling crates which displayed a dizzying variety of underwater creatures. So now we understood: the men catch the fish, tend the nets and boats, and the women dry and sell the fish.

As we prepared to leave Nazaré we felt somewhat sad to see these hardworking people living very much as they always had but with the twentieth century crowding in. How much longer would it last? Would they be happy to deal with change, or would it have an adverse affect on them? Time would tell.

Menu

ASSORTED OLIVE APPETIZERS
(PAGE 73)

POTATO AND KALE SOUP
(PAGE 83)

PORTUGUESE CORN BREAD (BROA)
(PAGE 77)

COLD MIXED SEAFOOD PLATTER
(PAGE 108)

GARLIC MAYONNAISE
(PAGE 72)

ROAST CHICKEN WITH PIRI-PIRI
(PAGE 138)

A Castle
by the Sea

IT HAD BEEN a long day. We got a late start out of Lisbon because of complications in trying to book passage on a car ferry to Morocco. In addition, we had lingered far too long watching, mesmerized, as workers stripped enormous sheets of cork from groves of cork oak trees. The area south of Lisbon is one of the primary cork growing areas of the world, and there are dark piles of it everywhere, on trucks, on the side of the road and in depots.

Now we were half way between Lisbon and the southern shore and wondering where we would find a hotel. There was a tiny "castle" symbol on our map at a place called Vila Nova de Milfontes. It marked a town on the coast at the mouth of the Mira River. We swung our car off the main highway onto a secondary road and continued several miles to a dusty town. Its main square was the only paved area, and we were quite sure that with the exception of a few campers, no one was going to find shelter here. We must have looked quite bedraggled from the heat as we made several inquiries. Yes, there was a hotel, we were assured—but where? Finally we spotted a tiny sign with an arrow pointing straight towards the one building we had overlooked. How could we have missed the biggest structure there? The castle was the hotel! A real castle with a moat and a draw bridge, it looked imposing standing grandly on a high point of land, overlooking the broad sandy delta of the river.

We approached the giant wooden front door and rather timidly lifted the door knocker. This did not look like a hotel: no name, no other cars. Our knock brought a response, though. A uniformed man opened the door and assured us a room was available and that it included all meals. Settled. Another man carried our two suitcases through a great hall, up some narrow stairs, and into a delightful room. High twin beds, some dark heavy chests and a writing table furnished it. Opening the window shutters revealed a flower-filled courtyard one floor below, and beyond that the river, as it made its way to the nearby Atlantic. Our escort announced dinner for eight o'clock and left. Wonderful! We had time to wash, rest, and explore a bit of the town. By seven we were starved and poking around the main living room. Several other guests had assembled and informed us that this hotel depended on word of mouth to fill the rooms. Port was offered. Payment seemed a bit vague. This was more like someone's home than a hotel.

We discovered a thirty-year-old guest book, filled with names, comments, a few photos, and cards. Fading fountain pen inscriptions, in that distinctive handwriting that Americans always identify as European, filled the pages, the occasional one written in English and testifying to a "lovely stay" or the "charming host."

Dinner was announced. The guests filed into a quite formal dining room, and as there were only six of us, we sat at one end of a long table. There were a Spanish couple, a French couple and ourselves, a strange group to have gathered one evening in July for dinner in a Portuguese castle. The French couple acted as translators for the group. Talk that evening rambled through discussions in three languages of bull fights, Paris, the economy, and, of course, the castle. We learned that the site had, in Carthaginian times, been a stronghold, later added to in turn by the Romans, the Moors, and the Crusaders. Then it was ransacked by Algerian pirates, and finally it was defended by the Spanish during their occupation of the area. Allowed to fall into ruin for four hundred years, it was eventually purchased in the late 1930s and transformed by the ambitions of one man into this charming hotel.

The hour grew late, and we made our excuses. Walking slowly back upstairs to our room, we reflected, as we often do when we travel, on the joy of chance events and people coming together to create the sort of perfect evening we had just experienced. The mellow mood was interrupted by our laughter at finding two chamber pots beneath our neatly turned down beds!

The next morning dawned crisp and blue. We awoke at eight to a knock from a maid with a breakfast tray of pastry, rolls and coffee. Finishing quickly, we were ready for a swim. There was a sandy beach that sloped up sharply from the water. The water was much lower this morning, indicating that this delta was tidal when the river water was mid-summer low. The clear water was surprisingly icy and shallow. We were able to walk halfway across. The morning was spent enjoying the sun and the refreshing river. High on its point of land, standing guard over it all—the town, the beach and the bathers, the river and the forest beyond—was the castle.

By noon we wandered back to be ready in time for the one o'clock main meal of the day. Now we were thirteen: six French, three British, two Spanish and ourselves, filling the single long table. Several waitresses in black uniforms and starched white aprons stood quietly. The meal was elaborate. A first course consisted of whole grilled fish and tomato salad, with white wine and delicious Portuguese bread. The large fresh fish was a surprise. It tasted like trout with a lovely smoky overtone from the wood fire. A second course of fried liver, sausage, and potatoes, and a dry red wine was followed by cheeses and quince jelly, and finally fresh fruit, dried figs, almonds and champagne. It was at about this point that we saw with absolute clarity the wisdom of the Mediterranean custom of the siesta. Prodigious amount of food and drink could produce a stupor that could only be remedied by a nap.

Conversation through this long and rambling meal was again conducted in at least three languages with the French couple never faltering in their translations. Unbelievably, everyone thought it a grand idea to have port in the living room; mercifully we needed to be on our way south, and by three o'clock we were leaving eleven strangers turned friends to sip and nap away the afternoon in a Portuguese castle by the sea.

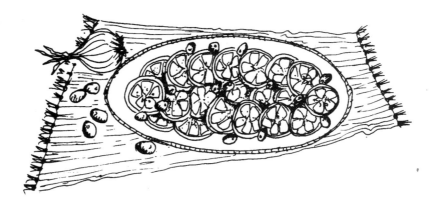

Menu

GRILLED TROUT
(PAGE 110)

PORTUGUESE COUNTRY BREAD
(PAGE 78)

LIVER AND SAUSAGE WITH FRIED POTATOES
(PAGE 126)

TOMATOES WITH MIXED GREENS SALAD
(PAGE 102)

QUINCE PRESERVES
(PAGE 155)

FIGS FILLED WITH ALMONDS AND CHOCOLATE
(PAGE 156)

An Algarve Lunch

———— —

THE ALGARVE REGION of Portugal, in the far south, is so isolated that it was treated as a separate kingdom under the crown until 1910. It is bordered by a range of mountains to the north, the Atlantic Ocean to the west and south, and the River Guadiana, forming its border with Spain, to the east. Quite small, perhaps twenty miles north to south and eighty miles long, it is like a lovely garden where winter hardly exists, and clouds of almond blossoms announce spring in January. Its climate is dry and mild, and the recent influxes of tourists are not the first to discover its charm. There is evidence of prehistoric settlements, and the Greeks and Phoenicians frequented its natural harbors, but it was the Romans who civilized it. Later, from the eighth through thirteen centuries, it was a flourishing and cultured Arab kingdom—indeed, the "al-Gharb," in Arabic, was the last Moorish stronghold on the European continent before the Christian re-conquest. At its southwestern most point, called Cape St. Vincent, lies the town of Sagres, where in 1420, Prince Henry established his famous school of navigation.

We planned to spend a few days relaxing on its beautiful golden beaches that lie at the foot of high ochre-colored cliffs. The spectacular rock formations spilling out into the water on several of them form secluded coves, perfect spots for swimming and sunbathing. With over fifty beaches indicated on our map, we knew better than to try to see them all, and besides, we knew that some of the real charm of the Algarve lay just inland in some of the tiny villages of old Portugal, untouched by tourism. We would allocate a good portion of our time to exploring them and the cuisine of the region.

We had taken a room in a small inn near the picturesque fishing village of Sagres and had gone that afternoon to visit the fortress and government-run hotel on the site of the old navigational school at Cape St. Vincent. The cape is a high windswept point of land jutting out into the ocean, an impressive reminder of the long-ago days when Portugal and her intrepid explorers took command of those waters. Later, we drove the short distance back for a swim at Praia da Rocha, known as the queen of the Algarve. It is an unusually beautiful beach bordered by cliffs and grottos.

That evening we found a restaurant that served a wonderful baked red snapper with roasted potatoes and a basket full of chewy bread. As we sipped our wine, we planned the next day. We would rise early and drive east on the main shore road, stopping in towns along the way that looked interesting, try to find a midday meal on the coast, and then head somewhat inland and drive the higher country roads back west, returning late in the day to our hotel.

The next morning dawned typically clear and dry. We were on our way by eight (tourists are hard-working souls), stopping for a simple breakfast in Lagos, an historic town that was the center of trade between Africa and Portugal and served as the capital of the Algarve from the sixteenth to the eighteenth century. German and Scandinavian tourists crowded into this sunny region. Portimao, ten miles further east and surrounded by many internationally known beaches, is another crowded playground, and we passed through quickly, crossing over the bridge spanning a natural harbor. Within minutes we were in the countryside and delighted in looking at the many sparkling white farm houses with blue window and door frames. Each had an Algarve style chimney that varied from house to house in its imaginative lace-like stone pinnacle. The beaches here were almost deserted, and we stopped for a walk and an up-to-the-knees wade. Back in the car we had to wait while two identical large-wheeled carts drawn by patient oxen crossed the road.

Our northern eyes had never before seen geraniums growing wild on large bushes but they, and bougainvillea vines, were everywhere. Just outside the next town of Porches we spied a small sign announcing Porches Pottery, and we turned in the gate along a pink stucco wall. The courtyard, which I immediately photographed, was full of bright pink bougainvillea, an old cart, and several enormous olive oil jugs. The entrance to the shop was framed in blue and white ceramic tiles, and inside, several women were painting beautiful images of birds, animals, and flowers on the pottery. The owner was a genial Irishman who told us that he had come here and helped to organize the local potters. The ware was striking, and we bought several pieces. Back in the car and still headed east, we traveled another thirty minutes or so into Albufeira, a bustling fishing and market town that still retains its Moorish character. Houses here are flat roofed and cut by open terraces at many levels.

Near the edge of town, several cars were parked at a restaurant. It was lunch time, and some families were already enjoying their meal when we walked in the door. After we settled at a table, a waiter came over and began motioning to us. We thought he wanted us to follow him, but his hand motions had a strange "go-stop" quality to them that confused us. In frustration, he finally took us by the arm and led us into the kitchen. Along one wall was a long fireplace, and on its top were eight or ten strange looking hinged copper vessels. Their round lids and bottoms were nearly identical, some open and some shut tight. Two cooks were tending them and several other pots, at another more conventional stove along the back wall. The waiter directed us toward the copper vessels, and it was clear by his encouraging look that we should choose one of them. We nodded, and went out to await our meal.

All the other patrons were eating, family style, from the bowl-like bottoms of the round pots. We thumbed through the food section of our guidebook and discovered that we were about to feast on an Algarve specialty: cataplana. Lunch arrived with a flourish, the waiter setting the cataplana (the name of the vessel as well as the food) on a hot plate and removing the pins that held the top lid in place. Delicious smelling steam cleared a bit to reveal a nest of about a dozen wide open clams and underneath, in a tomato-based sauce, cubes of pork. It tasted slightly sweet, and we soaked up every last bit of it with the bread. Later we learned that there are some variations, but most recipes for cataplana include shellfish, pork, ham, sausage, and tomatoes.

After lunch we continued east through Faro, an artistic center and the present capital of the region, to Tavira, an historic city that dates from the Roman period. There we spent an hour walking its quaint streets and photographing colorful boats on the river, before turning inland and west for the ride home.

Loulé is one of many picturesque and charming towns in the hills north of the coast. Old walls and monuments surround it. It's the handicraft center of the Algarve and worth a stop to watch craftsmen fashion harnesses, tin ware, ceramics, wrought iron—and cataplana! After our extraordinary lunch we had to buy one so that we could duplicate that meal at home. Happily clutching our handmade copper pot, we continued on our way to Silves.

Silves was the old Moorish capital of the Algarve until the 16th century and contains an interesting castle that we stopped to see. All the villages in this area are lovely, with gleaming white houses set among the orange groves. It was growing late as we began the final leg of our journey back to Sagres. We felt happy and enjoyed the sunset as we drove. It had been, perhaps, a day packed with too many things, but the Algarve is like that. Its beauty entices the visitor to see, taste, explore, buy, sunbathe, and swim to the point of happy exhaustion.

Menu

PORK AND CLAMS IN A CATAPLANA
(PAGE 127)
OR
BAKED RED SNAPPER WITH TOMATOES
(PAGE 115)
OR
COZIDA (PORTUGUESE BOILED DINNER)
(PAGE 137)

PEAS ALGARVE STYLE
(PAGE 96)

Old Lisbon

LISBON IS THE perfect capital for a country like Portugal. It is relatively small and can be enjoyed in several days of sight-seeing. But any city worth visiting is more than a collection of sights, and the quiet, civilized character of Lisbon is its real delight. It lies on seven low hills where the Tagas river broadens out into a large bay, before it empties into the Atlantic Ocean. Like most places on the European continent, it has a long history of human occupation, starting with the Phoenicians around 1200 B.C., followed by Greeks, Carthaginians, Romans, Moors, the Portuguese monarchy, and finally, the Republic from 1910 until the present.

Portugal's development into a 15th century maritime power made Lisbon a very important port, and one can see evidence of the riches that poured into the city in the elaborate stonework of her public buildings, monuments, and museums. It was the capital of the Portuguese empire and a world center for trade in spices, gold, and jewels.

As in most of coastal Portugal, the summers are warm and the winters mild, making Lisbon a perfect city for strolling. We had several days in June to spend there and decided to begin our sight-seeing by taking a taxi to the highest point, and coincidentally back in time to the site of the earliest settlement, the medieval castle of São Jorge—St. George—begun in the fifth century and added to by the Moors in the ninth century. Its ten towers stand on the hill where the original Phoenician colony was located. We were driven to a large courtyard shaded by many pine trees. An ancient mill wheel lay on its side, and several young boys were using it as a table to extract pine nuts from the cones that fell from the trees.

The view of the city below—the bay with its majestic suspension bridge and in the near distance the Alfama district—was worth the ride. We wandered through the walkways, gates and gardens of the castle, its ancient passageways tranquil and inviting in the summer breezes.

The Alfama district directly at the foot of the castle consists of a warren of narrow twisting streets, often so steep that they include steps, and the district tumbles down the hill toward the docksides of the broad Tagus river. It is the oldest quarter of Lisbon; its Moorish style whitewashed houses and shops crowd the cobblestone streets where all living seems to take place. It is home for sailors and fishermen, old women dressed in black, and young boys who play soccer in the squares near the fountains from which their mothers draw water. Ground floor doorways open into restaurants and shops. Many houses are decorated with azulejos—blue and white tiles—and wrought iron balconies are bright with flowers. We wandered the labyrinth and finally stopped for our midday meal at a tiny restaurant with four tables set out in the sunshine at its door. Moments after ordering the caldeirada—a classic Portuguese fish soup—two steaming bowls arrived along with bread and beer. The scent was of tomatoes, olive oil, and garlic, with large chunks of fresh white fish in the rich broth. It was delicious, a perfect mix of ingredients where seafood is king.

The day was breezy and mild, good for a stroll, and we decided to take the afternoon to walk back to our hotel. We knew it to be several miles, but we also knew that there was much to see along the way. Down at the waterfront, we turned west and walked along the harbor until we reached a beautiful square called Terreiro do

Paço. Turning north, we entered the Baixa (or main shopping district), which was crowded with shoppers and business people. Looking down one side street, we saw women waiting to take an elevator up to the aptly named Barrio Alto (the high district) which lay on a hill to the west. Traffic was heavy on the one-way streets of this compact area, but finally at its northern end it opened up into the enormous plaza known as the Rossio, which was lined with cafés starting to come alive with late-afternoon customers.

At the northern end of the rectangular Rossio is the beginning of the beautiful Avenida da Liberdade, Lisbon's broad, handsome version of the Champs Elysées. It runs straight as an arrow for about a mile, tree lined and shady, its sidewalks made up of thousands of small colored cobblestones set in intricate swirling patterns. It was peaceful and cool, and we sat for a while on a well placed park bench, one of many that line this graceful avenue. Our hotel was just another two streets further, but we wanted to savor the early evening.

Later, back at our hotel, we knew there was one more place we had to visit that day which was typical of Lisbon: a fado club. Most are located either in the Alfama or Barrio Alto. We asked the proprietor of our small second floor hotel, a genial man who spoke very little English, for his recommendation. He was so definite in his choice of clubs and had been so helpful on other occasions that we decided with no further ado to take his advice. We took a taxi up to the Barrio Alto and entered a charming restaurant. It was an intimate wood-paneled place with a tiny floor level stage. It was early for the singing to begin, and we asked for the dinner menu. We chose a chicken soup with lemon and mint, and roast pork with piri-piri. The Portuguese have a special way with pork, often creatively combining it with shellfish, and roasting or braising it with one of many sauces. This version had a spicy hot crust of red Angolan peppers and garlic. It was served with pan roasted potatoes, lots of bread, and a strong red wine.

When we were finished eating and still sipping our wine, a man with a guitar quietly seated himself on the stool on stage. A woman dressed in a simple dress and black shawl walked over to stand beside him; he played one or two cords, the room grew quiet, and with eyes closed, the woman began to sing. It is hard to describe the soulful sadness of the fado, sung in a strong but quiet voice. Although we could not understand the words, the message of lost loves, the pull of fate, and the tragedies of life came through in the music.

Later, hailing a cab outside the restaurant, we were jolted out of our reverie by a rather wild downhill ride through the deserted streets back to our hotel. The roller coaster ride broke the mood and left us laughing. We vowed to return someday to listen again to the sad, haunting fado—and we did—but the beauty of the music never touched us more deeply than that first time.

Menu

ROSELLA'S FISH CHOWDER
(PAGE 88)
OR
CALDEIRADA (PORTUGUESE FISH SOUP)
(PAGE 89)
OR
CHICKEN RICE SOUP WITH LEMON AND MINT
(PAGE 82)

ROAST PORK WITH PIRI-PIRI
(PAGE 139)

Rice, Salt and Fish

IT WAS THE early afternoon of a clear summer's day, and we were approaching Aveira from the north, taking secondary roads through the countryside on our way from Oporto. The land gradually grew flatter and became more marshy as we drove along. Taking bridges across several small rivers, we finally found ourselves driving narrow roads raised slightly above expanses of rice paddies. The fields of emerald green rice were beautiful, stretching—as perfect as putting greens—into the distance.

Aveiro is often called the Venice of Portugal and, indeed, the approach to both by car reveals striking similarities. Each is very old and stands on a totally flat landscape, and each is crisscrossed by canals spanned by low-lying bridges, plied by unusual boats, and lined with patrician houses. As we drove into town, the road began to parallel a canal. Unlike Venice, in which the buildings sit directly at the water's edge, this canal had a road along its length and was lined with unusual homes which looked like ornate versions of Amsterdam's canal houses. Each was different from its neighbors, a unique structure of perhaps three or four stories, built by a wealthy family. The street level floor on some of them was colonnaded, the main entrance rich with wrought iron and carved wood detail. Their facades were colorful, some of soft pinks, some tans, some covered with the blue and white painted tiles called "azulejos." Many had ironwork balconies at the windows, and most had a very high single window on a smaller fourth floor. We were sure it provided a lovely aerie from which to survey the landscape which stretched for miles to the distant sea.

In the canal at the town center bobbed brightly painted flat-bottomed boats with the same swan-necked bow as a Venetian gondola. They were much bigger though, designed to sail the lagoon beyond the town in search of eel and shellfish, as well as seaweed, which is used as fertilizer in the rice fields. We learned that these boats, called "moliceiro," compete each year to be selected as the finest and most beautifully painted in the fleet.

We chose a hotel on the main canal, and our room had its own tiny ironwork balcony from which to watch the business of the town. After settling in, we decided to drive the last few miles to the beach, which is separated from Aveiro proper by a meandering lagoon or "Ria." There are excursion boats that will take visitors through the immense stretches of silvery blue water, to see marshes full of rushes and water lilies and to watch the gentle movements of the sails of the moliceiros. We continued on for several miles, finally reaching a strand of white sand crowded with cars, beachgoers, shops, and hotels. As we have many times before we tried to imagine this ancient town, lagoon, and beach as they were hundreds of years ago, full of wildlife, quiet, and peaceful. The 20th century is not always a welcome intrusion! The beaches of Barra and Costa Nova are beautiful, though, with their backs to the lagoon and their shores facing the Atlantic waves. The sun was beginning to dip over the ocean as we drove back, and we turned our thoughts to dinner.

Another broad avenue—this one with a tree-filled center island running its length—led east from our hotel into the heart of the commercial district. We took a long window-shopping stroll, and after about an hour, our appetites were keen. Aveiro has its own version of caldeirada (or fish stew) which always contains eel and shellfish and is flavored with cumin. Big steaming bowls of it eaten in a delightfully clean and charming restaurant were followed by a long walk back to our hotel. We had read that the culinary specialty of Aveiro was its sweet egg desserts. Earlier we had passed a few sweet shops that displayed a variety of them. They all looked like elegant jewels, but the most intriguing was called "ovos moles," a smooth yellow confection packed into a tiny wooden barrel with a little paddle provided for eating it. At a sidewalk café there was a similar display of variations on the ovos moles theme. This confection of egg yolks and sugar can be eaten as is, as a filling for cakes and marzipan, or as a sauce for puddings. Settling at a table outdoors in the soft breeze, we ordered port wine, and, unable to make up our minds, we rather greedily ordered three desserts! It was fun to sip and sample: a hedonistic end to an agreeable day.

The next morning dawned cool and misty. We drove back along the road we had taken the day before. We watched men, ghost-like in the mist, harvesting salt from the lagoon. They repeatedly raked it into piles at the edges of hundreds of rectangular salt pans. Each was small and shallow, new supplies of salt filling it with the incoming tide, and each was carefully harvested by skimming. At regular intervals, stretching into the distance as far as the eye could see, were ten feet high pyramids of salt. We stopped the car and watched the unusual sight for quite some time. A part of this harvest of salt is used to preserve the cod that the fishermen of Aveiro— in much bigger boats than their moliceiro—net from as far away as Greenland. "Bacalhau" (or codfish) preserved in salt is one of the mainstays of the Portuguese diet and has been for hundreds of years.

We began to think about the self-sufficiency that has been the special pride of Aveiro since the Middle Ages. The rice and vegetable farming is sustained by the seaweed fertilizer, the bounty of the lagoon and sea is preserved when desired by the salt from the bay, and the people grow rich enough on their commerce to build and ornament their unusual boats and homes. It is a lovely and quiet area, somewhat isolated in the midst of marshes, fields, rivers, and lagoons. Leaving town that day, we made one more stop—to purchase two tiny wooden barrels and the delectable confection within.

Specialties of Aveiro

OVOS MOLES
(PAGE 149)

ALMOND CAKE WITH OVOS MOLES
(PAGE 150)

PUDIM FLAN
(PAGE 147)

SWEET EGG CAKE WITH ALMONDS
(PAGE 151)

SWEET EGG CAKES IN SYRUP
(PAGE 148)

Mansions:
Past and Present

THE WEATHER WAS quite hot the day we decided to visit the Roman ruins at Conimbriga which lie a short ten miles south of the university center of Coimbra. The summer heat was unusually oppressive that week, and we wanted a respite from the city which had become dryer and dustier with each day.

The site at Conimbriga was inhabited even earlier than the Roman period, but it is the remains of the second and third century city that draws visitors today. If one spends time in virtually any country in Europe, one is struck by the far-reaching power and sheer size of the old Roman empire. The Romans, above all, were builders. Roads, towns, aqueducts, and temples seem to lie around each turn, and many present-day cities boast a slightly crumbling amphitheater, or a still-in-service bridge. Our interest in these signposts of history never seems to pale for us, and so again we found ourselves driving through a lovely valley to visit the Roman town at Conimbriga.

There is a small museum to be seen first, which provides an orientation to the site, a view of some artifacts that archaeologists have found there, and to our delight, a model of the main structures as they appeared 2,000 years ago.

The ruins are probably the most complete on the Iberian peninsula, and during its three hundred year active history, it was a place of great beauty. We walked the old Roman road a short distance from the museum into the ancient town and began to wander along the lanes and sidewalks. Most of what can be seen today are low walls, beautifully preserved mosaic floors, fountains, and columns. The high walls and roofs have long since disintegrated, but as we explored, it did not take too much imagination to picture the Roman citizens going about their daily chores or relaxing in the lovely, fountain-filled homes of the wealthy.

One house in particular—laid out in the Roman fashion with a central courtyard—had extraordinary mosaic floors, all in perfect condition. The pictures of garlands and flowers, people, animals and myths were created from thousands of tiny tiles in tones of red, ochre and yellow. The guard watched as we set to work snapping pictures of the floor designs. Then, with a friendly smile, he motioned to us to wait a moment as he ducked around a corner to turn a spigot that activated perhaps a hundred small fountains. They arched up and across into a narrow pool that encircled the courtyard. How completely lovely this home must have been for its occupants: a cool oasis of plants, columns, fountains and mosaics.

Further away, near some walls built later to repel the barbarians, archaeologists have uncovered the shallow graves of several people. Their bones now lie, somewhat less than peacefully, under sheets of plastic, open to the gaze of hundreds of tourists, exactly as they were interred two thousand years ago.

The sun was merciless at the nearly treeless site. After about an hour it was time for us to try something a little cooler. We decided to drive a few miles north of Conimbriga. There, at a place called Buçaco, is a majestic and tranquil forest. It was created hundreds of years ago and has been carefully cultivated and tended for centuries, at first by Benedictine monks, later by priests from Coimbra, and, finally, from 1628 on by Carmelite monks. A great wall has been constructed to surround and protect the 250 acre preserve and its monastery, and it is said, to keep out women. But today, roads and gates welcome all visitors to wander the tranquil groves of maples, cypress, cedars, and oaks, and to view the varieties of ferns, laurels, magnolias, and hydrangea and the over 700 varieties of exotic plantings from all over the world.

Entering the gates is like entering a primeval world of towering trees and quiet glades. The road winds endlessly upward toward the mountain top and at every turn there are clearly marked walking trails leading to chapels, grottos, and cloisters. Crowning the hill and housed in a former royal hunting lodge is a very special hotel. It is a fine example of an architectural style unique to the Portuguese, called Manueline. Named for King Manuel, this style is extremely ornate, reminiscent of the Gothic, and a perfect showcase for the wealth of the Portuguese empire in the 1500s. Its main staircase contains the most elaborate azulejos we've ever come across, rising nearly two stories up into the stairwell. We wandered through the main hall, peeked into the sitting and dining rooms, and then at the far side found a perfectly beautiful dining loggia. Imagine an open porch, all stone tracery, green plants, and sunlight, with a dozen round tables set for lunch. The high vaulted ceiling and pointed arch windows give one the impression of being in a combination of a Gothic cathedral and a greenhouse. Diners enjoy a view of the sumptuous Buçaco gardens beyond.

Outdoors, a long wisteria arbor in full bloom and buzzing with bees forms one edge of the elaborate system of hedges and brilliant flower beds on the hotel grounds. We strolled meticulous gravel paths through the garden and then walked the short distance to an interesting natural spring that has been tamed to cascade down over one hundred stone steps to a reflecting pond surrounded by magnolias. What a bucolic paradise is contained within these old walls!

The third in our trio of mansion visits had to wait until the next day when we drove south to Pena Park. This park lies in a densely forested and misty mountain area near the coast just north of Lisbon, and at its highest point is the Pena Palace. Once again we began a long drive up through a cool forest to reach the palace. Built about 150 years ago for the Portuguese monarchy, the architecture is most unusual. It is an almost comical combination of Baroque, Gothic, Moorish, and Manueline architectural styles. Every inch is covered by elaborate stone gargoyles, filigree, nautical motifs, and tracery. Inside, we entered room after room of equally elaborate gold leaf, mirrors, carvings, crystal chandeliers, and tapestries. It seems that King Fernando II and his queen could exercise no restraint in their enthusiastic construction of this palace.

From the terraces around the building one has a panoramic view of the forest below and the distant Tagus river, the Salazar Bridge, and the Atlantic coast. On the stone retaining wall, in a small alcove, sits a beautiful silver sundial, but this particular day was one of those rare overcast days in a Portuguese summer, and there was no shadow to tell us the time.

Turning around and looking up we saw a fantastic stone image. A half round room with three windows juts out from the gray walls of the palace, and appearing to be supporting it on his shoulders hunches a fierce-looking King Neptune. He is sitting, legs akimbo, in an enormous fluted shell, his flowing beard nearly touching the writhing sea serpents at his feet. Glowering eyes stare straight down at the people below. Our photo of him is one of our favorites.

A light rain was beginning, and it was becoming a bit chilly and windy as we left Pena Palace and drove down the mountain. The closest town is Sintra, and there we chose a small restaurant on a narrow side street for our dinner. Giant shrimp with red peppers, braised lamb with sausage, and later a dessert of sweet rice custard with cups of strong coffee tasted just right. We felt snug inside, as the rain continued outdoors. We sat for nearly an hour, lingering over glasses of Madeira and some fig and almond confections, and plotting our course for the next day.

Menu

SHRIMP WITH SWEET RED PEPPERS
(PAGE 117)

BRAISED LEG OF LAMB WITH SAUSAGE
(PAGE 133)

SWEET RICE CUSTARD
(PAGE 146)

ALMOND AND FIG BONBONS
(PAGE 157)

A Pousada
Fit for a Queen

DISCOVERING THE POUSADAS added a delicious new dimension to our continuing adventure in Portugal. Pousadas, (literally inns) were begun in 1940 by the government to provide a network of fully restored castles, monasteries, and mansions designed to provide reliable accommodations for the traveler. In the past fifty years, over thirty of these wonderful links with the past have been developed. Each one is unique and retains the character of the original building. Each is also a showcase of the regional architecture, crafts, antiques, and food. Pousadas are more or less evenly distributed across Portugal, and many are so extraordinary that they become the goal of that day's travel. We've stayed at a few and visited and eaten in many more. The opportunity to dine on authentic regional food in a beautiful room of a restored castle or monastery is not easy to pass up. By European standards, as first-class accommodations, they are still a bargain, and they are the stuff of which fantasies are made. Very often the pousada can be glimpsed from a distance—it's the castle on the mountain, or the fortification on the bluff, or the monastery next to the cathedral! As one approaches, it's impossible not to begin to daydream of the days when Crusaders battled Moors, when valiant knights protected the beautiful queen in the castle, and when cloistered monks and nuns began another day with their morning devotions.

The pride that the Portuguese people have in these bastions of old-world charm shines through from the moment one arrives. Depending on the season, they are either cozy and welcoming against the chill winds or a cool and tranquil haven from the summer sun. We have never been in one that did not have beautifully appointed public rooms and wonderfully helpful employees. One immediately has the feeling of being pampered and that a delightful evening is assured.

One of our favorite pousadas is at Estremoz. The day we had planned to stay there began hours earlier in Evora, an ancient walled town nearly two thousand years old, and a distance perhaps of thirty winding mountain roads from Estremoz. We had come there to see the Roman temple in the square and the great cathedral of this provincial capital. The town itself is wonderful for strolling and retains a distinctly Moorish quality in its streets and homes. Archways and flower-filled balconies line the cobblestone streets, and white buildings hide tiled patios and secret gardens.

It was a market day, and the town square was bursting with carts and stalls shaded with awnings. Household goods such as baskets, kitchenware, tools and clothing were for sale, but it was the handicrafts that drew us into the crowd. The Portuguese excel in this area, and our home is full of craft items from many such markets. Our first find was a large basket bought from a leather-faced man who was working on a mate to it. Now we had an excuse to buy more to fill the basket. In quick succession, we bought table mats, a ceramic water jug, and finally a small blue and white lidded ginger jar. All went into the basket.

In the south corner of the square and spilling into the side streets were the vendors of fruits and vegetables, spices and olives, sausage, breads, and cheeses. The fruit of sunny Portugal is outstanding, and we bought two of the biggest peaches we have ever seen. Into the basket they went, along with a small loaf of golden bread from another stall. Further down a narrow lane an old woman was selling her homemade sheep's milk cheeses, some wrapped in grape leaves and some in small straw baskets. She flashed her gold-toothed smile as we bought one for our lunch.

We walked back to the Roman temple for a second look. It is rather small and stands alone in the center of the town square. Gray Corinthian columns are still stately and graceful, although it is roofless now, two thousand years after its dedication to the goddess Diana. At the other end of the square is the cathedral; its mixture of styles—from the Gothic to Renaissance to the Baroque—attests to its construction which spanned almost four hundred years.

Our basket was heavy, and we were growing hungry. Retracing our steps past the temple, we continued across the square, around a corner and into a small park. A few shade trees and a stone bench were perfect for a picnic of fresh cheese, bread, and two very juicy peaches. We felt as if we had taken a bath in their juice, until we found a fountain to wash in.

Before leaving Evora we stopped to walk through a former convent transformed into a pousada. Each pousada is a special one-of-a-kind hotel. This one is directly across from the Roman temple and contains a lovely tranquil cloister at its heart.

An hour later, as our car neared Estremoz, we could see, high on the hill, the castle that was to be our hotel for the night. Slowly climbing higher and higher, the road at last ended in a huge courtyard surrounded by a wall and watchtowers. Several small boys practiced their soccer moves as we admired the windswept view of the valley below.

Great wooden doors surrounded by ornate stone carvings opened into a soaring lobby. We were led up a massive staircase and along a balcony corridor to our room. It was beautiful, furnished with antiques, and as the bellboy opened the enormous shuttered window, we heard and saw hundreds of swallows as they dipped and swooped by. This was the castle of King Dinis and his queen, Saint Isabel of Aragon, built in the 13th century and waiting patiently to be restored to this wonderful hotel.

After a restorative rest, we walked through the hallways and public rooms, feeling as if we were in a museum as we viewed the paintings, armor displays, lovely ceramics and massive pieces of antique furniture. The dining room was beginning to fill with other guests as we entered.

The menu of each pousada is as much a hallmark of its region as is the decor. There was much to choose from, and we finally selected a tomato and bread soup, a main dish of roast pork with figs, some side dishes of braised carrots and potatoes fragrant with coriander, and for dessert an orange pudding and a sweet cheese tart. The service was an embodiment of old-world elegance.

It was too early to turn in, and we opted for a stroll through the old town on the hillside and into the newer town below. Some children were in band uniforms and we followed them to an area near a large square where they and others began to form up for a parade. We settled onto a bench with anticipation and were treated, fifteen minutes later, to what has to be the world's shortest parade. We never did discover the cause for the celebration and returned to the castle laughing.

It had grown late, and we were among the last to return. As we walked to our room, a uniformed maid jumped to her feet and stood outside our door. She opened the door, showed us the turned down bed with a chocolate on each pillow, and, with a curtsy, asked us if there was anything else we might need. With this final touch, now we really did feel like the former residents of our castle, King Dinis and Queen Isabel.

Menu

TOMATO AÇORDA
(PAGE 85)

ROAST PORK WITH FIGS
(PAGE 140)

ROAST POTATOES WITH OLIVES
(PAGE 99)

BRAISED CARROTS
(PAGE 92)

ORANGE CUSTARD
(PAGE 145)
OR
ALMOND CHEESE TART
(PAGE 152)

A Town
Devoted to Pottery

WE HAVE A particular love of blue and white ceramics, and our home is full of a collection amassed over the years. The most classical examples of Portuguese blue wares are made in Alcobaça, a town about fifty miles north of Lisbon. We decided to make time for a detour to this charming town to search for a pair of candle-holders for that bare spot on our dining room table. Besides, we reasoned, Alcobaça's real attraction was its magnificent cathedral and monastery, which we planned to visit. We also intended to check out a restaurant just off the central plaza which supposedly specialized in the preparation of bacalhau, the classic salt cod of Portugal.

Alcobaça lies in a valley surrounded by wooded hills at the confluence of the Alcoa and Baca rivers. Eight hundred years ago, the Cistercian monks of the area began growing fruit here, and the orchards of the region are famous to this day.

All streets lead to the vast central plaza, and the wares of the pottery shops—thousands and thousands of blue and white pieces in every conceivable shape—spill out onto the wide sidewalks. At the far end, watching over the tangle of visitors and traffic is the tranquil facade of the cathedral. We left the car on a side street and began the delightful search for the perfect candle-holders. Pitchers, casseroles, planters, platters, cups, tiles, wall sconces, sculpture—the choices seemed happily endless. Not daring to skip even one shop we wandered carefully through a forest of pieces. The second floor of one shop was devoted solely to azulejos, the blue and white tiles that decorate walls everywhere in Portugal. We couldn't resist the temptation and bought a set of eight that we later had placed into a frame.

Earlier we had eyed one stately pair of candle-holders and had seen none we liked better. We hoped they would still be there. They were, standing almost fifteen inches high, their bases painted with intricate scenes of animals in a bucolic landscape. Flowers wind up the sculpted stem to a top that flared out to catch the wax drips. We loved them, and they were wrapped by the proprietor with great care for our airplane trip home. Several months after our return we saw similar ones advertised in a New York department store at nearly four times the price.

Locking our purchases in the car, we went in search of the restaurant about which we had been told. We found it on a street sloping up from the plaza. It was packed to overflowing, and as we waited for a table we looked at the menu. For centuries the Portuguese have preserved the cod caught off the Grand Banks of Newfoundland by salting, and large, stiff, cream-colored slabs of it are sold in every grocery store and fish market. The menu selections were almost entirely made up of some of the three hundred and sixty-five reputed variations of bacalhau or salt cod. Although many tables held tourists, local families with children, parents, and grandparents filled over half the restaurant. Happy, noisy, and with a wonderful aroma, this place fitted our state of mind after our purchases.

A table was finally free, and we took it. We had been observing that very few people ordered anything from the menu, but instead motioned to the busy waitresses who were continually circulating with large flat pans held high over their heads. These waitresses would scoop generous portions of the food onto plates and refill when requested. It appeared that there were several choices. We each ordered a simple sliced tomato salad and then somewhat arbitrarily selected food from two different waitresses. One dish was the classic Bacalhau à Gomes de Sá, a casserole of cod, eggs, and fried potatoes. We sampled from each other's plates and discovered they were both delicious. Refills were urged on us, and we ate until we were stuffed. Because of the long soaking and simmering required to begin any bacalhau recipe, all traces of salt are gone when its served, and it tastes like the freshest of fish.

After such a hearty lunch, we needed a walk and some on-our-feet sight-seeing. We crossed the plaza to the cathedral and monastery. The front facade is a Baroque addition, but upon entering, all is majestically simple. White columns soar almost seventy feet to a vaulted Gothic ceiling. It was hushed and cool inside, and we walked down the 350-foot long aisle to view the intricately carved tombs of the tragic lovers Inês and Dom Pedro. She was a lady-in-waiting to the wife of the king's son, Dom Pedro, and they fell hopelessly in love. She was killed for her transgression, and now their tombs rest together near the main altar.

To the left of the cathedral are the cloisters and monastery of the monks of the Cistercian order. The tranquil cloister garden is a perfect square, surrounded on all sides with two stories of columns and arches. Beyond it lies the great kitchen of the monastery which once had a branch of the Alcoa river routed through it so that the monks could fish for their dinners!

Later, after visiting the monastery, we walked to a nearby fruit market to buy some plums: fully ripe burgundy-colored ones. We ate them on the spot, trying not to let too much of their juice run over our hands and onto the street. Climbing into the car, we continued on our way, smugly satisfied with our purchases in the attractive town of Alcobaça.

Bacalhau Variations

A Remnant of the
Age of Exploration

—————

THE BEACH AT Figueiro da Foz, about one third of the way down
the coast of Portugal, has to be one of the widest white sand beaches
in the world. It stretches so far out from the main boulevard along
its length that the ocean cannot even be glimpsed. Long board-
walks march straight out across its width, and each day with the
blind instincts of lemmings, we carried our blanket, chair, lunch,
and books the long distance to the unseen water. We were spending a few days soaking up sun and salt water, trying some of the
many varieties of fresh fish the area is noted for and catching up
on our reading.

After spending much time in Portugal, we were curious to learn
more about her golden age of exploration and discovery, a 150
year period from about 1410 to 1560. During that brief span, Portugal dominated commerce and acquired great wealth. Under the
leadership of Prince Henry the Navigator, her brave explorers
pushed the edges of the known world. As every schoolchild learns,
the explorers' efforts were motivated by a desire to secure routes
of trade to India and the Far East. Each voyage planned by Prince
Henry reached out further and further from their little land, at
first leading to the discovery of the islands of the Azores and
Madeira in the Atlantic, and then advancing along the African
coast. By 1488 Dias had rounded the Cape of Good Hope, and

ten years later Vasco da Gama had reached India. Brazil was discovered in 1500, and by 1520 Magellan had sailed around the globe. Every new area, every new landfall, was claimed for Portugal. Fortified trading outposts such as Goa and Macao were established, and the stage was set for a fabulous and seemingly endless stream of riches to pour into the country. A shift of world commercial power from the Mediterranean to Atlantic ports—especially Lisbon—followed. The sea routes were safer than the overland trade routes, and from all over Europe goods flowed into Lisbon to be traded for the spices, gold, ivory, and jewels from the western hemisphere, Africa, and India.

Such wealth was ultimately damaging. Population began to fall as people migrated to India, farming and production declined, and the gold was used to buy food and goods from northern Europe. By 1575 the glory days were over, and Portugal quietly returned to her old ways. The traces of that glorious 150 years, however, are still found in her arts, architecture, and literature. Lisbon itself still has many Manueline style buildings with their unabashedly exotic Oriental and nautical motifs.

The effects of Portugal's contact with other lands and cultures are, of course, noticeable in its cuisine, which has incorporated such items as rice from the orient, hot peppers from Angola , cinnamon, cloves, and ginger from India, and the New World products of potatoes, tomatoes, and cod from Newfoundland. The palette of the country was changed forever, and this imprint is still much in evidence today.

On our third day in Figueiro da Foz we needed a break from our self imposed routine of reading and swimming. That afternoon we drove several miles north to the town of Buarcos, an old fishing village of medieval style houses protected by a thick beach front wall. During the 1600s, the people of Buarcos were harassed by pirates and built the long fortification that stands to this day. It was pleasant to walk the wall and visit two small churches there.

Later back in Figueiro da Foz—a much less quiet and more tourist-filled resort—we headed for the new quarter near the Mondego river. This busy port is made up of a yacht harbor for pleasure boats and a fishing boat harbor and shipyards for its cod and sardine fishing industry. Extending back from the harbor are many walking streets and handicraft shops. We browsed for a while, looking at ornaments of shell and coral and some furniture and weaving created by local artists. The streets were crowded with tourists, tanned and relaxed after their days on the beach.

The hour was growing late. We had passed one particular restaurant earlier and decided to return to take our evening meal there. It was very small, and the sign announced it as Goan. After reading about the old Portuguese trading enclave at Goa, on the west coast of India, we were curious to taste the result of several hundred years of culinary experimentation. From the enclave's inception the spices of India were incorporated into Portuguese cooking and remain there to this day, but what about the effects of Portuguese cuisine on Goa? Would the people of Goa, many descendants of Portuguese who came in the 1500s, retain distinctly Portuguese foods but combine them with Indian ingredients?

We left our dinner choices in the hands of the genial proprietor who charmed us with his smile and, unlike many Portuguese, spoke English. He guided us through a meal that included a shrimp curry and a delicious chicken and potato dish served with a delicately flavored fragrant rice. A small arranged salad with a light dressing of lemon juice, salt, and a dash of cayenne pepper, and an unusual eggplant salad were soothing counterpoints to the spicy curry. For dessert we were served little coconut and almond cakes.

We savored every bite of the complex and subtle tastes, many unfamiliar to us. We took careful notes, but it was only upon our return home, with the help of a friend—Esther Saldanha, who was raised in India—that we were able to duplicate the recipes we tasted that evening. Esther can trace her (and her husband's) family history back for hundreds of years in Goa, and all five recipes are from her family cookbooks.

It is said that the development of a cuisine is as certain an indicator of historical events and the migrations of people as are, for example, language and art. That evening in Figuero da Foz, we had an enjoyable meal, but much more, we discovered a hybrid, a unique and subtle blending of tastes which was a sure marker of Portugal's age of exploration and discovery.

A Goan Dinner Menu

SHRIMP (OYSTER) CURRY
(PAGE 111)

JEERA MEERA MASALA
(PAGE 135)

EGGPLANT SALAD
(PAGE 104)

FRAGRANT RICE
(PAGE 101)

LETHRI
(PAGE 154)

The Costa Do Sol

THE COAST OF Portugal juts out to form a small peninsula to the west of Lisbon, and several of this small country's more interesting sights lie on it, within an easy drive of the city. Setting out early one morning, we stopped for breakfast in Caracavelos, a pleasant resort town with wooded campsites and a sandy beach.

The Portuguese have a high regard for their special coffees, a taste acquired from coffee growing possessions and former possessions such as Brazil, Angola, and Mozambique. Even though it was quite early in the day for the serious afternoon business of sipping a favorite blend at a coffee shop, we followed our noses to one establishment already brewing individual aromatic cups for each customer. After selecting our coffee, we chose several small breads and pastries and sat at a table just outside the door to enjoy the passing scene and plan the day.

We would continue west to the resort towns of Estoril and Cascais, enjoy the views at Praia do Guincho and Cabo da Roca, turn inland and east to visit Sintra, and further on, Queluz, before returning that evening to Lisbon. The whole coast is a resort area known as the Sun Coast or Costa do Sol, but a few towns manage to retain a bit of their older fishing industries.

Leaving Caracavelos, we found the traffic on the main coastal road becoming heavy. We drove less than ten miles further to Estoril, a fashionable, international resort town. The climate is considered to be particularly fine here, and this day was no exception, with its clear sky and gentle breezes. Estoril was, until recently, a small spa, attracting visitors to its healing waters, but it has now developed into a first-class—and beautiful—resort. We intended to spend an hour or so strolling its tropical gardens, its fine sand beach, and the lovely Cascais Bay area. All was in full bloom, and the wide esplanade in front of the casino was particularly stately, lined with palms and planted with beds of pink and red impatiens.

Later, a very short drive west brought us to the vacation resort of Cascais. Archaeologists have found evidence that prehistoric man also appreciated the mild climate and magnificent sheltered bay of the region, and it has been constantly occupied since, as a fishing village. The real turning point for Cascais occurred about one hundred years ago when the Portuguese royal family chose it as a summer retreat, inducing a steady stream of aristocrats to also build their homes there. Today the town's harbor plays host to large yachts, small pleasure boats, and fishing vessels, and manages to blend old customs with the new tourism.

Our "harbor hobby" has always been to ogle the big boats, look at their ports of origin, and vicariously make the journeys they have. And so we passed a pleasant hour wandering along the waterfront, before deciding to eat a light lunch of tomato and sausage soup at one of Cascais's excellent small restaurants.

The road out of Cascais cuts south around the peninsula, and within a mile one approaches an area known as the Jaws of Hell. Here, especially when the sea is rough, the water is forced between two rock formations where it crashes and sprays impressively. This day was calm, and only one or two other cars had stopped to view the spectacle. After a while we continued our drive around the end of the peninsula and started north.

This province is called Estremadura, and inland it is a region of gentle hills and small villages where orchards, vineyards, and olive trees share land with corn and wheat. Along the coast, rocky cliffs that tumble into the sea alternate with beautiful sandy beaches. As the road turned north around the peninsula, we stopped first to view the vast beach at Praia do Guincho. A few miles further the sandy beach rises a towering five hundred feet to a cliff called Cabo da Roca. It is Europe's westernmost point. We parked the car and slowly walked the path to the edge of this sheer cliff over the sea. The calls of hundreds of sea gulls flying below carried up to our ears over the sound of the pounding surf. The wind tore at our clothes, and the lovely wild flowers were reduced to growing only an inch or two above the ground. Standing there looking out at the vast Atlantic Ocean, we could sense, as we had on other occasions, the lure that it must have had on the Portuguese of hundreds of years ago, both terrifying them and enticing them to explore—daring them to drop off the edge or to sail on to distant harbors in a world without edges.

From the cape the road leads inland and through the sleepy village of Colares, known for its dry red wine. We continued driving through winding mountain roads and climbed higher and higher through a series of switchbacks until we finally reached Sintra. It is a mountain town and differs completely from the towns of the coast and rolling plain below. The relatively high elevation in the area traps the Atlantic mists, and the generous rainfall nourishes exotic vegetation. It has been called a glorious Eden, and, indeed, we found ourselves in a town of walled villas, lush gardens, and small homes and shops that seemed to cling to the very sides of the mountain itself. Narrow twisting roads led us, on foot, through the oldest parts of the village.

On an earlier trip we had visited the unusual Pena Palace there, but we had not been to the nearby Moors Castle. After enjoying the cobblestone streets and small shops of Sintra, we drove the short distance to the castle and climbed the steps in the tower. The view of the town, the forest, Pena Palace—and, in the distance—

the coast, was unforgettable. The castle is over a thousand years old, built during the Muslim occupation of Portugal and has watched over the peninsula since that time.

Leaving Sintra, we followed the highway about ten miles southeast to Queluz, a town best known for the eighteenth century palace that was once home to the royal family. A beautiful pink rococo building, it is surrounded by statues, fountains, lakes, and gardens. On a tour of the interior we gaped in awe at the painted ceiling, opulent furnishings, priceless art, and other trappings of royalty that have earned this palace the label of the "Portuguese Versailles." It was growing late, and although the gardens and lakes beckoned us to spend more time, we instead decided to drive the final ten miles back to Lisbon. We promised ourselves to return again.

Having planned earlier to take a ferry across the Tagus river to enjoy dinner at one of the small seafood restaurants there, we first returned to our hotel to rest. It had been a lovely but long day, and we were tired. Several days earlier a chance acquaintance had suggested either driving the magnificent Salazar Bridge or going by boat to enjoy the view of Lisbon from across the river.

Later, emerging onto Avenida da Liberdade from the hotel and hailing a taxi we were at the waterfront in minutes. It had turned cool and windy, especially on the water, but in a short time we were on the other side. Even from the dock we could see several possibilities, and a quick walk brought us to a rather new, clean restaurant selected for its view. A waiter showed us to a seat at a window. Lisbon, which is surely one of the loveliest capital cities in Europe, stretched before us. Viewed from a distance it is all pastels and ochre, flowing over its seven hills, and crowned by the majestic castle of St. George.

One of our favorite dishes is deep-fried squid prepared the way it is done in Portugal, and we ordered it along with potatoes and a pepper salad. For our appetizer we decided to share some grilled prawns. Washing this down with a dry white wine, we watched as each of the seven hills in succession gave up the light of the setting sun, and as each section of the city slowly lit itself against the night.

We had to hurry later to catch the last ferry. On the dock, shivering in the night air, we were lucky to find one last taxi to return us to our hotel. We marveled again at the variety of experiences we had packed into one day—beaches and mountains, castles and palaces, windswept capes and lush forests. This is truly a nation in miniature, a country of contrasts. It is said that Portugal is Europe the way it used to be—certainly this is true of its capital, too.

Menu

TOMATO AND SAUSAGE SOUP
(PAGE 84)

GRILLED SHRIMP
(PAGE 116)

DEEP-FRIED SQUID IN BATTER
(PAGE 113)

TWICE COOKED POTATOES
(PAGE 100)

MIXED PEPPER SALAD
(PAGE 103)

Obidos—
A Fortified Town

"YOU MUST SEE Obidos," we were told. "It is unforgettable." So one day we drove the sixty miles north along the coast from Lisbon. The high crenellated walls and castle of this ancient fortress are visible many miles before reaching the town. It sits like a ship at the crest of a high hill, and in the centuries before the bay at its feet filled with silt, it guarded a busy harbor. Today Obidos sits six miles inland and the once-deep bay is a calm, shallow lagoon full of fish and waterfowl.

A twisting portal guards the entrance to the walled town. We decided that parking the car outside was much wiser than attempting to drive the serpentine turns of the gate. Walking through, we looked up two stories in the guard tower to see overhanging openings from which, long ago, soldiers could protect the town's entrance from invading armies. Once inside, we stepped back hundreds of years into a world detached and isolated from the present.

One main cobblestone street, several side streets, and cross lanes were lined with sparkling whitewashed houses. Flower boxes dripped with geranium, and walls were covered with bougainvillea vines. We began our slow stroll uphill toward the one thousand year old Moorish castle at its crest. At every turn there were shops to peek into, doorways and window frames painted clear blue, red, or yellow in the Portuguese manner, charming court-yards, and a few steps leading from house to house. From every vantage point one could see the high stone walls surrounding the tile-roofed buildings.

Obidos has an interesting history. Built by the Moors, it was won back by the Portuguese monarchy in the 12th century. From the 13th century on, the town, its walls, and the castle have been bestowed by each king as a wedding gift to his queen.

Many small shops along our way had local craftsmen sitting in the doorways working on items such as wrought iron pieces and handwoven rugs. The rugs, especially, we found attractive, and we bought a small cotton one from the old gentleman who created it.

The streets wound around past the neat homes, and local house-wives went quietly about their chores. How lovely it must be to live in such a place. At the very top of the steepest street, set in the midst of lush bougainvillea, is the thick Gothic archway leading to the castle. The Portuguese government has turned this ancient monument into a pousada or inn, for travelers. All pousadas have fine regional fare in their dining rooms, and the Pousada do Castelo is no exception. The room was fit for royalty with a high-beamed ceiling, blue and white tile azulejos on the walls, a fireplace, and windows deep enough to hold a table for two. It was early, and we were happy to be given one of these tables. The window had elaborately carved stone frames in the Manueline style and commanded a view of the valley below. We ordered a rich roast suckling pig with juicy crackling skin and some chicken braised in red wine, sampled each other's choices, and pronounced them fine. We ended the meal with a refreshing fruit compote.

After lunch we walked into the courtyard and finally up an enormous staircase to the main hall of the castle. Massive antique pieces of furniture, charming paintings, and shiny suits of armor were everywhere in the museum-like pousada.

Later, we finished our explorations of the labyrinth of small streets and squares and took picture after picture of pretty window gardens, quaint doorways, and small courtyards. Obidos is a photographer's paradise!

Back in the main square, we sat for a while on a stone bench built into the cobblestone wall and watched the owner of a grocery shop pile lush peaches and purple plums with infinite care into an attractive display. A child with a cart, two more playing ball, and a housewife carrying her string bag to the market made up a scene that looked so ordinary that we wondered how many times it had been repeated in this unusual place. For over a thousand years people have been living in this perfectly preserved niche of antiquity, its houses fitted just so within its protecting walls.

To the left, next to the guard tower, a steep flight of steps, tight against the wall, leads up to a walkway that encircles the fortification. With some trepidation we climbed the stairs to the top and began to walk the narrow path. It was unprotected, and several running young men showed off their teenage bravery to each other. Our pace was a more prudent slow walk, sticking close to the outer walled side. At each crenellation, perhaps six feet apart, one could glimpse the valley below. From the inside edge one could look down onto the rooftops, trees, and tiny vegetable gardens of the residents. Rounding a corner and starting up the long side, we caught a glimpse of one of the hundreds of working windmills of the region as it turned slowly in the wind. The setting sun cast long slanting shadows over the angles of the wall, giving the stones a golden glow. Below, nestled in its arms were the red-roofed white houses of Obidos. The person who had sent us here was right: it was unforgettable.

Menu

TRIPE—OPORTO STYLE
(PAGE 129)
OR
CHICKEN (OR RABBIT) BRAISED IN RED WINE
(PAGE 131)
OR
ROAST SUCKLING PIG
(PAGE 142)

BROAD BEANS WITH BACON AND SAUSAGE
(PAGE 95)

FRESH FRUIT COMPOTE
(PAGE 144)

Lisbon—
The Waterfront

LISBON IS PORTUGAL'S most exciting city, and after several visits and many days, there were still more sights to see. It was from Lisbon's harbor, in use for three thousand years, that explorers in the 1500s left to sail the seas to discover new lands and bring back gold, spices, and jewels. The Tagus river spreads out to form a large bay at the foot of the seven hills of the city, and along this waterfront are several "must-see" monuments. We decided to take a taxi to the farthest, the Belém Tower and spend the day visiting it, the Hieronymite Monastery, the Monument to the Discoveries, and several museums.

We sped down the Avenida da Liberdade, around the Rossio to the river, and then along the broad harbor-front highway toward Belém. Summertime in Portugal is the season that enjoys almost perfect weather, and another clear, blue day was beginning.

Belém Tower is a severe looking, five-story, gray-stone building, which when it was built in 1515, stood in the middle of the river. It now sits at the water's edge, because the river has changed its course. It was from this historic site that the caravels of Vasco da Gama, Alvares Cabral, and other brave explorers were launched to begin their explorations. At the corners of the square tower are round sentry boxes where guards stood watch over the harbor and scanned the horizon for returning ships. It stands today as a proud reminder of Portugal's glorious past. For a small fee we were allowed to climb the stairs, walk the terraces, and view the world from its tiny balconies.

A short walk back toward the city and across the avenue is the enormous Hieronymite Monastery. It was built in the 1500s at a time when untold riches were pouring into Lisbon from its territories. The monastery is probably the best example of Manueline architecture. Fantastically intricate and beautiful stone carvings adorn every surface, inside and out, both within the church and its adjoining cloister. We were in awe of the interrelated power and wealth of the church and government in the 16th century.

In sharp contrast, directly across from the monastery, on the waterfront, is the Monument to the Discoveries. Built in 1960 to honor Prince Henry the Navigator, it stands in a vast mosaic plaza that depicts a map of Portuguese world discoveries. Its clean modern lines represent the bow and sails of a giant stylized ship. At the prow stands Prince Henry, and behind him, all eyes fixed on the horizon, stand several dozens of Portugal's most illustrious citizens and valiant explorers.

From there, a walk along the waterfront took us to a pleasant restaurant with a half dozen outdoor tables. Our flight home was very early the next morning, so we decided to eat our big meal in the afternoon and only take a snack before an early bedtime that evening. We began with a large plate of cold marinated mussels, and later ordered a shellfish açorda—a thick and filling soup that always contains bread. Fried potatoes and some cauliflower with a zesty sauce completed our feast.

After lunch we walked back to the Maritime Museum, housed in a wing of the monastery, to look at displays of five hundred years of Portuguese ships and ship models. It is hard to believe that such precarious looking wooden vessels with their huge sails could have completed those long-ago journeys to unknown destinations.

The day had been a long one, and our intention was to begin to walk toward the city and watch for a taxi or trolley. A small building on the river advertised a museum of folk arts, and we couldn't resist. It had just opened, and no listing of it was in our guidebook. It was fresh and new and had a wonderful display of the arts, crafts, and tools of the Portuguese country people, past and present. The entire collection could be viewed in under an hour, and it delighted us in a way that older, richer, and bigger museums seldom have. We were surprised by how little change there might be in the design of a well conceived tool over hundreds of years and how the craft items of an area also remain constant.

Later we were lucky to find a taxi within minutes of leaving the folk museum. Back at our hotel, we showered, packed, paid our bill, and left instructions for a dawn wake-up call. It was dusk when we walked out onto the Avenida da Liberdade and down two blocks to a small restaurant where we ordered a type of cold quiche or egg pie, washed down with some beer. We strolled the lovely avenue and then finally had some coffee and shared a sweet pastry at a café down a side street. We would miss Portugal, Lisbon in particular, but were excited by our plans to begin a book to share our experiences and recipes with others.

Menu

MARINATED MUSSELS
(PAGE 107)

SHELLFISH AÇORDA
(PAGE 86)

COLD EGG PIE WITH PEAS AND SAUSAGE
(PAGE 97)

CAULIFLOWER WITH PIQUANT SAUCE
(PAGE 93)

Cabañas, Nazaré.

Fish market, Nazaré.

A fisherman mending his nets, Nazaré.

Fishing boats, Algarve.

Seacoast, Algarve.

Scene along the Avenida da Liberdada, Lisbon.

Salt harvest, Aveiro.

Fishing boats (moliceiro) used in the lagoons around Aveiro.

Sunset in Aveiro.

Royal hunting lodge, now a hotel, at Buçaco.

Roman mosaic floor, villa at Conimbriga.

Houses and castle, Obidos.

Flower vendor, Coimbra.

Woman returning from the public market, Coimbra.

Recipes
of Portugal

Sauces
Appetizers
Breads

Garlic Mayonnaise

An all-purpose mayonnaise for cold fish, this recipe is simple to make in a blender.

1 egg
1 teaspoon ground mustard
¾ teaspoon salt
¼ teaspoon piri-piri or dash of cayenne pepper
¼ cup olive oil
3 cloves of garlic sliced thin
3 tablespoons lemon juice

Put these ingredients into a blender. Cover and blend thoroughly. Remove the cap on the pouring opening in the lid of the blender and while it is running, very slowly pour in:

1 cup of olive oil.

Makes 1½ cups. Refrigerate. Keeps one week.

Olives in Garlic

It is a rare restaurant in Portugal that does not immediately present diners with a small dish of marinated olives. Grocery stores commonly devote much shelf space to a large variety of them. Olives come in a wide range of sizes and colors, from deepest black to pale tans, rich golds, purples, and greens. Try this duo of appetizers as a perfect start to a Portuguese meal. They keep for several weeks under refrigeration.

  30 to 40 black olives, preferably Calimata
   1 red chili pepper
   3 garlic cloves
  ¼ cup olive oil

Drain olives. Cut chili pepper into small pieces and discard seeds. Mince garlic cloves. Combine all four ingredients. Cover and chill for several days.

Olive Appetizer

1 large can of green olives with pits, drained
6 pepperocini peppers, drained
½ cup celery, coarsely chopped
1 small onion, chopped
1 teaspoon oregano
1 bay leaf
2 tablespoons capers, drained
2 tablespoons vinegar
½ cup olive oil
   salt, pepper to taste

With a small sharp knife make several cuts in each olive. Slice pepperocini peppers into several large pieces each. Combine all ingredients, mix well. Cover and refrigerate for several days, mixing once each day.

Piri-piri 1

Piri-piri is the hot seasoning oil of Portugal, with as many varia-tions as there are housewives. It is added to all manner of meat and fish dishes, soups, sauces, marinades, and stews, but it is fiery and to be used with caution. Prepared in advance, piri-piri will keep under refrigeration for months.

¼ cup fresh hot chili peppers
2 garlic cloves, minced
½ teaspoon salt
1 cup olive oil

Coarsely chop the peppers, discarding the tops. Thoroughly wash hands, knife and cutting board afterwards.

Combine peppers, salt, garlic, and oil in a glass bottle. Cover tightly, refrigerate. Use as needed.

Piri-piri 2

¼ cup fresh hot chili peppers
1 cup olive oil
1 slice of lemon, quartered
1 bay leaf
½ teaspoon salt
½ cup of brandy or whiskey
2 cloves of garlic, minced

Coarsely chop the peppers, discarding the tops. Combine all ingredients in a small sauce pan and simmer gently for 15 minutes. Cool and pour everything into a glass container. Cap and refrigerate. Use as needed.

Portuguese Corn Bread (Broa)

Not like American corn bread, it is often served with potato and kale soup.

   1 package active dry yeast
   1 teaspoon sugar
1¼ cups warm water
   ¾ cup warm milk
   1 teaspoon salt
   1 tablespoon olive oil
   2 cups yellow cornmeal
   3 cups all-purpose flour

In a small bowl mix the yeast, sugar and ¼ cup of the water.

While that sits, mix the remaining water, milk, salt, oil and corn-meal in a large bowl. Add the yeast mix, stir, and then slowly add the flour to make a soft dough that is not too sticky. Add a bit more or less flour as needed.

Turn out onto a floured surface and knead for 5 minutes. Place in a greased bowl, cover, and allow to rise in a warm place for one hour.

Punch down, knead again for 5 minutes, then form into a round loaf. Place in a greased 9-inch pie pan, allow to rise again until double in bulk, about one hour.

Bake in a preheated 350° oven for 40 minutes or until the loaf sounds hollow when tapped. Cool on a rack.

Serves 6.

Portuguese Country Bread

This is the daily bread of the Portuguese countryside, served in every restaurant and home. It is delicious and has a wonderful crust. If it is possible to find a bread flour, use it instead of all purpose flour. The secret to the crust is the humidity in the oven.

1 package active dry yeast
1 cup warm water
1 teaspoon salt
4 cups unbleached white flour

In a large bowl dissolve the yeast in the warm water. Add the salt and then add the flour, 1 cup at a time. Mix the first cup vigorously with a wire whisk. After the second cup you will have to continue mixing with a wooden spoon and by the third cup and part of the fourth cup you will have to mix with your hands.

Add the last of the flour slowly and when it no longer sticks to your hands turn the dough out onto a floured surface and begin kneading. You may have to add a bit more flour to the surface as you knead to prevent sticking. Knead for 10 minutes. Place the dough in a greased bowl. Cover. Let it rise in a warm place until double, about 1 hour.

Punch down, knead an additional 5 minutes. Form into an oval loaf, place on a greased cookie sheet. With scissors or a razor blade, snip or slice several cuts in the top. Let rise again until double, about 45 minutes.

Bake in preheated 350° oven for 30 minutes. Twice during the first 15 minutes of baking, open the oven door and spray a bit of water into the oven from a clean atomizer bottle (or place a small pan of boiling water on lower shelf for the baking period).

Cool finished loaf on a rack.

Serves 6.

Soups

Chicken Rice Soup with Lemon and Mint

This delicate soup is popular all over Portugal, and the combined scent of lemon and mint is delightful.

2 quarts of canned chicken stock
1 medium onion, finely chopped
⅓ cup uncooked rice
1 whole chicken breast
 juice of ½ lemon, about two tablespoons
 several large sprigs of fresh mint
 pepper
 lemon slices

Pour the stock into a large saucepan, add the onion, rice, and chicken breast. Simmer for 30 minutes and remove the chicken.

Pull the chicken off the bone and cut into strips. Return it to the stock along with the lemon juice.

Remove enough leaves from the mint to make ¼ cup chopped. Add the mint and some ground pepper to the stock. Simmer several minutes to heat through.

Serve garnished with thin lemon slices and additional mint leaves.

Serves 6.

Potato and Kale Soup

This soup, served everywhere in Portugal today, is originally from the north. A wonderful winter offering, it is so typical of much of Portuguese cooking: hearty and fragrant. It is traditionally served with a kind of corn bread called "broa" (see page 77).

⅓ cup olive oil
1 medium onion, chopped
¼ pound of garlicky smoked sausage such as chourico, linguica or keilbasa, sliced
3 medium potatoes
6 cups water
½ pound of kale or collard greens
salt

Place oil in a medium skillet and sauté with the onions and sliced sausage. Set aside.

Peel and slice the potatoes and cook in the water until quite soft. Mash into the water.

Slice the kale as thinly as possible into very fine julienne threads. Add to the potatoes and water. Simmer for 5 minutes, add the reserved sausage, onions, and oil. Heat through for 1 or 2 minutes. Do not overcook. Salt to taste.

Serve immediately with broa.

Serves 4.

Tomato and Sausage Soup

This hearty summer soup requires the best vine ripened tomatoes. If these are not available, canned tomatoes are a fine substitute. Plan to serve the soup with lots of bread: the Portuguese way is to place the bread in the bottom of each bowl and pour the hot soup over it.

2 tablespoons olive oil
½ pound chourico (spicy pork sausage), sliced
2 medium onions, sliced
1 pound or 1 can ripe tomatoes
5 cups canned chicken stock
1 bay leaf
½ cup chopped parsley
   salt to taste
1 small red or green chili pepper (chopped) or 1 teaspoon piri-piri (see page 75)

In a saucepan heat the oil over medium heat, and brown the sausage and onions until the onions are golden. If you are using fresh tomatoes, peel and chop them before adding them to the sausage and onions. If you are using canned tomatoes, pour them with their liquid into the pot with the sausage, and break them up with a spoon.

After cooking them for five minutes, add the stock, bay leaf, parsley, salt, and chopped chili or piri-piri. Simmer gently for 30 minutes.

Serve with or over bread.

Serves 6.

Tomato Açorda

Açordas are Portuguese soups that always include bread in them.
They are thick and hearty, a meal in themselves. One like this is
a specialty of the Pousada da Rainha Santa Isabel in Estremoz.

⅓ cup olive oil
1 cup sliced onions
1 tablespoon minced garlic
1 28-ounce can of whole tomatoes including their liquid
1 tablespoon fresh oregano or 1 teaspoon dried oregano
2 bay leaves
¼ cup chopped parsley
1 49-ounce can of beef broth or 6 cups fresh beef broth
  salt and pepper to taste
1 loaf of crusty French bread
  eggs, one per serving

In a large saucepan, heat the oil and lightly brown the onion and garlic. Add the tomatoes and their liquid, oregano, bay leaves, and parsley. Break up the tomatoes and simmer for 10 minutes.

Add the beef stock and simmer, uncovered, for one hour. Stir occasionally. Add salt and pepper to taste.

Before serving, cut one thick slice of bread per serving and place in the bottom of each soup bowl. Gently break the eggs into the simmering soup to poach for about 5 minutes. Spoon some soup and one egg over the bread in each bowl.

Serve with additional bread.

Serves 8.

Shellfish Açorda

An açorda is a Portuguese style soup that always uses bread slices or bread crumbs to add thickening and body. This is similar to the one we were served at a small restaurant along the river in Lisbon (see "Lisbon—The Waterfront"). It is more of a first course than a soup.

2 dozen cherrystone clams
  stale French bread
½ cup olive oil
1 tablespoon minced garlic
4 cups chicken stock
⅓ cup chopped parsley
  salt and pepper to taste
½ pound of small raw peeled shrimp
4 eggs
  lemon wedges for garnish

Steam clams in a large covered pot until they just open. Remove them from their shells and discard any that do not open. Set aside.

Cut the crust off the bread and crumble 3 cups. Heat the olive oil in a large skillet and cook the garlic until golden. Add the bread. Toss it to coat with the oil and garlic. Fry until it is crisp. Set aside.

In a deep saucepan, heat the chicken stock and add the parsley, salt, and pepper. Add the shrimp and clams to the stock. Gently break the eggs on top of the simmering stock. Cover and simmer very slowly for about 5 minutes or until the shrimp are pink and the eggs are just set.

Lift out the eggs to a dish, and divide the broth and shellfish evenly into four soup bowls. Divide the fried bread crumbs over the fish in each bowl. Top each portion with a poached egg.

Serve at once with lemon wedges.

Serves 4.

Rosella's Fish Chowder

Soups using fish (caldeiradas) are predictably common in the Portuguese cuisine. This version comes from Rosella Lopes.

1 tablespoon olive oil
1 large onion, chopped
1 can of whole tomatoes plus liquid
1 teaspoon salt
3 small potatoes, peeled and cut into cubes
4 cups of water
2 pounds of fresh cod fish cut into cubes
2 teaspoons vinegar
    pinch of saffron

In a large saucepan, heat the oil and add the onion. Brown slightly and add tomatoes, salt, potatoes, and water. Simmer for 20 minutes.

Add the fish, vinegar, and saffron. Simmer for an additional ten minutes or until the fish and potatoes are cooked.

Serves 6.

Caldeirada (Portuguese Fish Soup)

This caldeirada contains a variety of fish and shellfish, and, with a salad, makes a complete meal.

    4 tablespoons of olive oil
    1 large onion, chopped
    2 cloves of garlic, minced
    1 green pepper, seeded and chopped
    1 can of whole tomatoes plus its liquid
    1 bay leaf, crumbled
    1 cup of dry white wine
    3 cups of fish or chicken stock
    1 teaspoon piri-piri (see page 75) or hot red pepper flakes
    2 pounds of mixed fish fillets such as cod, haddock, snapper,
      etc., cut into cubes
    2 dozen cherrystone clams in their shells
    1 loaf of crusty Portuguese style bread
    ½ cup of fresh coriander or parsley, chopped

In a large saucepan heat the oil and slightly brown the onion. Add the garlic and green pepper and heat for another minute. Add the tomatoes and their liquid, the bay leaf, wine, stock, and piri-piri. Simmer for 15 minutes, then add the fish pieces. Cook for 5 minutes, add the clams and cook for 5 minutes longer.

In the meantime, cut a thick slice of bread per person and place one in the bottom of each broad soup bowl. Ladle the broth with its fish over the bread. Garnish with chopped coriander or parsley.

Serve with additional bread and a white wine (see "A Word About Wines").

Serves 6.

Vegetables
and Salads

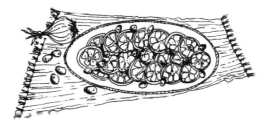

Braised Carrots

These buttery carrots were served as part of a formal meal at a pousada we stayed in (see "A Pousada Fit for a Queen"). Ours were cut into thin rounds, but set your creativity to work on another elegant trim.

½ stick of butter
2 onions, finely chopped
8 carrots, peeled and sliced
⅓ cup of orange juice
3 whole cloves
   salt and pepper

In a medium saucepan with a tight-fitting lid, melt the butter and very slowly cook the onions, uncovered, until they are soft but not brown. Add the carrots, orange juice and cloves. Toss to coat with the butter and onion mix, cover, and braise over very low heat for about 20 to 25 minutes or until the carrots are just tender.

Check once or twice and add a tablespoon or so of water if the orange juice has evaporated. There should be no liquid left at the end, and the carrots should be covered with a sweet fragrant glaze. Add salt and pepper to taste.

Remove the cloves and serve hot.

Serves 6.

Cauliflower with Piquant Sauce

Vegetables in Portugal are virtually never served "as is." Portuguese cooks most often use a delicious combination of ingredients to enhance the taste of their vegetables.

Vegetable:
- 1 cup water
- 1 head of cauliflower, trimmed and broken into flowerets
- ½ cup flour
  salt and pepper to taste
- 2 eggs, beaten
- 1 cup unseasoned bread crumbs
  vegetable oil for frying

Heat one cup of water in a deep lidded saucepan. Put the cauliflower flowerets into the pot and steam over high heat without lifting the lid for 5 minutes. Drain cauliflower and allow to cool.

Place the flour, salt, pepper, and cauliflower into a plastic bag, close the top, and gently shake to evenly coat the vegetable. Shake off the excess flour, dip each piece in turn into the beaten eggs, and then roll in the bread crumbs.

Heat enough oil in a large heavy skillet to hold a single layer of breaded cauliflower. Fry on one side for 3 minutes, turn each piece once and fry for 3 minutes on the other side or until golden. Continue until all pieces are fried.

Drain on paper towels and keep warm.

Sauce:

- ½ cup olive oil
- 2 cloves garlic, minced
- ½ teaspoon piri-piri (see page 75) or ¼ teaspoon hot red pepper flakes
- ¼ cup white wine vinegar
- salt to taste

Heat the olive oil in a small saucepan and cook the garlic until golden. Allow to cool off the heat for a few minutes, then add the piri-piri or pepper flakes, the vinegar, and salt. Return to the heat to simmer for 1 minute.

Pour this sauce over the cauliflower and serve.

Serves 6.

Broad Beans with Bacon and Sausage

Broad beans—similar to lima beans—are an often served vegetable in Portugal. Traditional cooks long ago discovered broad bean's affinity to bacon and sausage. Most recipes for them are variations on this popular theme.

¼ pound chorizo or other garlicky smoked sausage
¼ pound sliced bacon
1 medium onion, chopped
2 tablespoons olive oil (if needed)
½ teaspoon ground cumin
1 pound shelled broad beans or lima beans
¼ cup each, chopped parsley and coriander
½ cup chicken broth
    salt and pepper to taste

Cut the sliced bacon into small pieces and fry for several minutes in a large skillet with a lid. Cut the chorizo into small pieces and add to the bacon. Add the onion and sauté for several more minutes.

Add up to 2 tablespoons of olive oil if the bacon does not yield enough of its own fat. Add the cumin. Put the beans, parsley, coriander, and chicken broth into the skillet, bring to a boil, reduce to a simmer, and cook covered about 15 minutes or until beans are tender.

Test seasoning, and add salt and pepper if necessary.

Serves 4.

Peas Algarve Style

Vegetables in Portugal are seldom just steamed. Often they are slow-cooked with other ingredients such as oil, onion, garlic ,and bits of sausage to create memorable counterpoints to more simply cooked meats and fish. This version of peas from the Algarve is typical (see "An Algarve Lunch").

2 tablespoons olive oil
1 medium onion, chopped
1 sweet red pepper, cut in strips
¼ pound linguica, chourico, or any garlicky smoked sausage, diced
1 pound frozen peas
½ cup water
¼ cup fresh coriander (or cilantro) chopped
salt and pepper to taste

In a lidded skillet or saucepan, brown the onion in the oil, add the pepper and sausage, and cook for 3 minutes more. Add the peas and water. Lower the heat, cover tightly and simmer for about 15 minutes or until the peas are tender. Add coriander, salt and pepper to taste.

Serves 4.

Cold Egg Pie with Peas and Sausage

Similar to quiche, pies like these are often offered cold for lunch or warmed as a first course at dinner.

Crust:
    1 cup all-purpose flour
    ¼ cup vegetable oil
    2 tablespoons milk
    ¼ teaspoon salt

Put the flour into a small mixing bowl. Mix together the oil, milk, and salt, and pour into the flour. Mix lightly with a fork until just incorporated.

Form into a ball and then roll out between two pieces of waxed paper until it fits a 9-inch pie pan. Remove the top piece of waxed paper, lay the crust upside down into the pie pan and carefully strip off the second piece of paper. Trim and crimp the edges. Bake in a 350° oven for 8 minutes or until set. Cool.

Filling:
    1 cup frozen peas
    ¼ cup olive oil
    1 onion, peeled and chopped
    ⅓ pound chourico or linguica sausage, peeled and crumbled
    ¼ cup parsley, chopped
    4 eggs
    1 cup milk
    salt and pepper to taste

Cook the peas for 10 minutes in boiling water. Drain.

In a skillet, heat the olive oil, add the onion, and lightly brown. Add the sausage and cook for 3 minutes. Add the drained peas and parsley. Cook for 1 minute and set aside to cool.

Beat together the eggs, milk, salt, and pepper.

Spread the sausage and peas mix into the bottom of the baked pie shell. Pour the egg and milk mix over the sausage and peas and place the pie pan into a 350° oven. Bake for 40 minutes or until the eggs are set.

Cool before serving.

Serves 4 to 6.

Roast Potatoes with Olives

These delicious potatoes are an easy accompaniment to any roast, and can be cooked in the same oven as the meat (see Roast Pork with Figs, page 140).

5 or 6 potatoes, peeled and quartered
⅓ cup olive oil
1 large garlic clove, minced
    salt and pepper to taste
⅓ cup slivered Calimata olives
⅓ cup chopped parsley

Toss the potatoes in the olive oil, garlic, salt, and pepper. Arrange in a single layer in a roasting pan. Place in a 350° oven for about 45 minutes or until roasted through and easily pierced with a fork. Turn pieces once or twice during that time so they don't stick, and so that they develop a golden all-over glaze.

During the last several minutes of roasting time, toss them with the olives.

Serve hot with parsley sprinkled on top.

Serves 8.

Twice Cooked Potatoes

The Portuguese are not as calorie conscious as we are and these potatoes were served to us with deep-fried squid (see "The Costa do Sol"). They are absolutely delicious but might be more suitable served with a lightly grilled meat or fish.

2 pounds boiling potatoes of fairly uniform size
4 tablespoons butter
4 tablespoons olive oil
⅓ cup chopped coriander
    salt and pepper to taste

Cover the potatoes with water in a large pot and cook over medium high heat until done, about 30 minutes. Drain and let cool. Slip off the skins and cut each potato into four pieces.

Heat the butter and oil in a large skillet. Add the potatoes and gently turn them over medium high heat until they turn golden. Sprinkle with coriander, salt, and pepper.

Serves 6.

Fragrant Rice

Basmati rice has a natural nutty perfume unlike any other. Look for it to make this typically Goan dish.

  1½ onions, chopped
    1 tablespoon butter
    1 inch of stick cinnamon
    4 whole cloves
    1 teaspoon salt
    1 clove garlic, minced
    ½ teaspoon ginger powder
    2 cups basmati rice, rinsed once and soaked for 5 minutes
  3¾ cups boiling water
    ½ teaspoon ground turmeric

In a deep lidded saucepan, sauté the onions in the butter. Add the cinnamon, cloves, salt, garlic, and ginger. Gently fry for 1 minute.

Drain the rice and add it to the spices. Toss to coat with butter.

Measure 3¾ cups of boiling water into the rice mix. When it returns to boiling, add the turmeric, reduce the heat, and simmer for 15 minutes.

Shut off the heat and leave rice covered for 5 more minutes before serving.

Serves 6.

Tomato and Mixed Greens Salad

This salad, featuring tomatoes, requires only the best red, vine-ripened, summertime kind!

¼ cup olive oil
1 tablespoon wine vinegar
¼ teaspoon salt
¼ teaspoon ground pepper
   mixed greens such as bibb, endive, Romaine, watercress and Boston lettuce, washed, dried and torn into bite size pieces
1 or 2 large tomatoes, thinly sliced
1 small red onion, thinly sliced and separated into rings
10 black olives, preferably Calimata

Combine the oil, vinegar, salt and pepper. Pour half this dressing over greens and toss gently to mix. Place greens on a flat platter.

Arrange the tomatoes in overlapping slices on top, then the onion rings, then the olives. Drizzle the remaining dressing over everything.

Serves 4.

Mixed Pepper Salad

When we were served this salad at a riverfront restaurant, (see "The Costa do Sol"), all the peppers were green, but we think it would look especially attractive if red and yellow peppers were combined with the green.

2 green bell peppers, peeled and seeded
2 yellow bell peppers, peeled and seeded
2 red bell peppers, peeled and seeded
⅓ cup olive oil
1 clove garlic, minced
salt to taste
6 pickled pepperocini peppers

To peel and seed peppers: Place peppers in a roasting pan and heat under the broiler, turning frequently, until they begin to blister. Take out of the oven and cover the pan with foil. Allow to cool.

With a sharp knife pull the thin skin off the peppers. Cut open, remove the stem and seeds, and cut each pepper into 8 or 10 long strips.

Mix together the oil, garlic and salt. Slice the pepperocini peppers into small sections, remove their seeds and stems, and put them into the oil. Pour this dressing over the bell pepper pieces in a large bowl. Toss lightly to coat, cover, and refrigerate for several hours.

To serve, arrange on individual plates.

Serves 4.

Eggplant Salad

An unusual salad, we ate one similar to this as a vegetable side dish (see "A Remnant of the Age of Exploration").

1 large eggplant
2 onions, chopped fine
¼ cup vinegar
1 hot green chili pepper, minced
1 teaspoon minced fresh ginger
1 teaspoon sugar

Wrap eggplant in foil, prick once or twice with a fork, and bake for 1 hour at 350°. Cool, skin, and break up flesh with a fork.

Mix together onions, vinegar, pepper, ginger, and sugar. Add to eggplant. Chill for several hours.

Serve cold to accompany Goan curries.

Serves 4.

Seafood

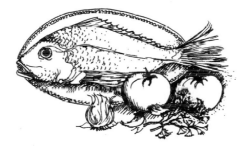

Marinated Mussels

These marinated mussels are simple to prepare ahead of time and make a fine appetizer along with a glass of chilled white wine.

    1 cup dry white wine
    4 dozen mussels, "beards" removed
  ½ cup olive oil
    3 cloves garlic, minced
  ¼ cup white wine vinegar
  ¼ cup chopped parsley
  ⅛ teaspoon ground black pepper
     salt to taste

Heat the wine to boiling in a large deep pot with a cover. Put in the mussels and toss them for a few minutes in the boiling wine. Then put the lid on and, over high heat, steam them until they just open. Discard the wine and any mussels that fail to open. Remove them from their shells and throw away the shells.

In a skillet, heat the olive oil and fry the garlic and mussels together for several minutes. Remove from the heat, add the vinegar, parsley, ground pepper, and salt. Toss to coat and place the mussels plus all of their marinade into a glass dish, cover, and refrigerate for one day.

Stir occasionally and serve cold.

Serves 4 to 6.

Cold Mixed Seafood Platter

This dish, served with garlic mayonnaise, (see page 72) is more a state of mind than an exact recipe. It was presented to us with several items such as edible barnacles that are difficult to find in this country. It should include at least some of the following:

- Lobster, crawfish or shrimp—cooked, shell-on and chilled
- Poached salmon or other firm fish—cut into pieces and chilled
- Steamed mussels or clams—one half of shell discarded, chilled
- Squid—cleaned, cut into rings and poached until just cooked

To cook the seafood—each separately—use these guidelines:

To cook shrimp: Heat to boiling in salted water, then lower heat and simmer gently until the shrimp turns pink, about 1 to 3 minutes

To cook lobster and crawfish: Same as shrimp with these times:
3 ounces each—for 3 to 4 minutes
6 ounces each—for 8 minutes
8 ounces each—for 11 minutes
whole 1½ pound lobster—for 20 minutes

To poach salmon: In a flat pan with a lid heat 1 quart water, 1½ tablespoons salt, and 2 tablespoons lemon juice to boiling. Add salmon steaks, simmer 10 minutes. Remove from water and drain. Chill.

To steam shellfish: Clean outside of shellfish with a brush if needed. Pull off the beards on mussels. Place over boiling water in a steamer. Steam for 6 minutes. Discard all unopened shellfish.

Arrange each variety attractively on a bed of lettuce, with lemon wedges and the garlic mayonnaise.

Serve: As individual appetizers or main dishes or on a large platter as a buffet offering. For main dish allow ½ pound seafood per person.

Grilled Trout

Grilled fish is as common in Portugal as grilled hamburgers are here. The Portuguese use fish that are about eight or nine inches long. Fresh trout is a good choice.

1 cleaned, scaled, rinsed and dried trout or other small
    whole fish per person
    olive oil
    salt and pepper
    lemons

Start the grill well ahead of time so that only glowing coals remain. The grill should be about 5 inches above the coals.

Rub the fish with olive oil inside and out, then sprinkle with salt and pepper. Brush the grill with additional oil. Grill the fish for about 5 or 6 minutes on each side. Turn carefully only once. They are finished when the juices run clear.

Serve immediately with lemon wedges.

Shrimp (Oyster) Curry

This recipe originates in the Portuguese colony of Goa on the west coast of India.

In Portugal we ate it as a shrimp curry, but our Goan friend Esther's family prefers this made as an oyster curry (see "A Remnant of the Age of Exploration"). Either way it is a favorite!

2 tablespoons vegetable oil
2 large onions, chopped
2 garlic cloves, minced
1 teaspoon fresh ginger, minced
½ teaspoon turmeric powder
½ teaspoon coriander powder
½ teaspoon cumin powder
2 hot green peppers minced or ½ to 1 teaspoon red pepper flakes or powder
4 cans oysters, drained (save the juice) or 1½ pounds peeled raw shrimp
2 large potatoes, peeled and cubed
1½ cups canned coconut milk
8 ounces plain yogurt
1 tablespoon lemon juice
Salt to taste

In a large lidded fry pan heat the oil and sauté the onion. Add garlic, ginger, turmeric, coriander, cumin and hot peppers. Cook on low heat for 2 minutes. Do not allow it to burn.

(If using oysters, add their broth), add potatoes and coconut milk.

Simmer covered until the potatoes are tender. Add yogurt and shrimp (or oysters) and gently cook until oysters or shrimp are just cooked. Do not overcook. Season with lemon juice and salt. Serve with *Fragrant Rice* (see page 101).

Serves 6.

Deep-Fried Squid in Batter

Squid, called "lulas" in Portuguese, is found on the menus of most small seafood restaurants, probably because of its quick preparation time. It takes three or four minutes to deep-fry; in fact, anything longer makes it tough. With a light batter, it is delicious.

1½ pounds uncleaned squid or 1 pound cleaned squid
1⅓ cups flour
  1 tablespoon olive oil
  2 well-beaten eggs
    salt and pepper to taste
¾ cup beer
    vegetable oil for frying

To clean squid: Cut off the head end including the beak-like mouth. Remove the ink-sack, turn the body sack inside out, and remove the transparent cartilage. Pull off any attached membranes and rinse well. Cut into ⅓ inch slices to form rings. Cut the six arms into portions. Dry all pieces thoroughly by rolling in a paper towel.

Batter: In a bowl, gently mix together the flour, oil, beaten eggs, salt, and pepper. Gradually add the beer. Do not beat the batter. Allow to rest covered in the refrigerator for at least one hour.

Preparation: Pour about one inch of cooking oil into a medium sized skillet. Heat to 375°. (A test piece coated in batter should cook golden brown in no more than 3 to 4 minutes.)

Put all the dry squid pieces into the batter and turn to completely coat them. Working quickly, pick pieces out, one at a time, and place into the hot oil. Do not allow them to touch or overlap. Continue frying for 3 to 4 minutes until they are golden brown and then scoop them out with a slotted spoon. Drain on fresh paper towels. Cook additional batches if necessary.

Serve at once with fresh lemon wedges.

Serves 4.

Baked Red Snapper with Tomatoes

Portugal's incredible wealth of seafood means that one is never far from fresh fish and the often simple traditional seafood dishes, such as this one.

 3 tablespoons olive oil
 2 onions, chopped
 2 cloves of garlic, minced
 ½ cup parsley, chopped
    salt and pepper to taste
 1 cup dry white wine
 4 to 5 canned red tomatoes, drained and chopped, or use an
    equal quantity of fresh ripe tomatoes peeled and chopped
 2 pounds of red snapper fillets

Preheat oven to 350°.

In a skillet, heat the olive oil and brown the onions and garlic, then add parsley, salt, and pepper. Add the wine and cook over high heat until it is reduced by half. Add the tomatoes and simmer for 3 minutes.

In a greased ovenproof dish large enough to hold the fish in one layer, spread half the tomato mix on the bottom, arrange the fish on it, and spread the remaining mix on top of the fish. Bake for 35 to 40 minutes or until the fish tests done.

Serve with *Twice Cooked Potatoes* (see page 100).

Serves 4.

Grilled Shrimp

Shrimp or prawns, called "gambas" in Portugal, are often served in the following manner. We ate them from small skewers that had held them for grilling (see "The Costa do Sol"), but an interesting variation is to cook them quickly in a skillet in their marinade and serve over rice as a main dish.

1½ pounds of peeled uncooked shrimp
4 tablespoons olive oil
2 cloves garlic, minced
1 teaspoon piri-piri (see page 75)
⅓ cup brandy
¼ cup chopped parsley
4 skewers

Combine all ingredients in a bowl, cover and refrigerate for several hours or overnight.

Divide shrimp into four portions and pass the skewer twice through each shrimp. Either broil or grill shrimp for several minutes on each side, turning once. Do not overcook. If using the alternate method of cooking, place shrimp and all the marinade in a large skillet and cook over medium high heat for 4 to 5 minutes or until the shrimp turn pink. Do not overcook.

Serve over rice.

Serves 4.

Shrimp with Sweet Red Pepper

Use large, fresh shrimp for this recipe and be sure to not overcook them. This recipe looks pretty and it's delicious. Serve it with steamed rice.

¼ cup of olive oil

3 cups of sweet red peppers, seeded and cut into 1 inch chunks

1 cup of chopped onion

⅓ cup of parsley, chopped

½ teaspoon of piri-piri (see page 75) or ¼ teaspoon of dried hot red pepper flakes

½ cup of Calimata olives, pitted and sliced

¼ pound of prosciutto or other cured ham, sliced

1 pound of cleaned, peeled, uncooked shrimp
chopped parsley and lemon wedges for garnish

In a large skillet with a cover, heat the olive oil and lightly brown the pepper pieces and the onion. Add the parsley, piri-piri, and olives. Cover and remove from the heat for 5 minutes.

Cut the prosciutto into two inch strips. Uncover and return the pan to high heat. Add the ham and shrimp and quickly sauté all for 2 to 3 minutes or until the shrimp turn pink. Turn out onto a bed of steamed rice.

Garnish with parsley and lemon wedges. Serve at once.

Serves 4.

Bacalhau

Bacalhau, dried salted cod, has been a mainstay of the Portuguese diet for over four hundred years. Even today, in the age of refrigeration, it is a preferred taste (see "A Town Devoted to Pottery"). It must be soaked for one or two days in several changes of water before preparing it in one of its hundreds of ways. It has a robust flavor and is always served with a red, rather than a white, wine (see "A Word About Wines").

Begin all bacalhau recipes by preparing the fish in this way:

Soak fish in water for at least 24 and preferably 48 hours, changing the water 3 to 4 times each day. Drain the bacalhau, rinse well, and place in a saucepan with enough water, to cover. Bring to a boil. If the water is too salty, drain, add more fresh water and bring to a boil again. Lower the heat and simmer for 20 minutes. Drain. When cool, remove any skin or bones, and separate the fish into coarse flakes. Continue from this point with any recipe.

Bacalhau à Gomes de Sá

This recipe is the most popular method of bacalhau preparation in Portugal.

1½ pounds bacalhau, prepared as outlined on page 118
  6 medium potatoes
  4 medium onions
 ¾ cup olive oil
  1 small clove garlic, minced
20 black Calimata olives, pitted and sliced
  6 hard-boiled eggs, shelled and sliced
 ¼ cup chopped parsley

Cook, peel and slice the potatoes.

Peel and finely slice the onion. Into a heavy skillet, pour ½ cup of the olive oil and the onions. Cook for 5 minutes, add the garlic and cook for 2 more minutes.

Brush the bottom and sides of an ovenproof casserole with oil. Assemble by spreading half the cooked potatoes on the bottom, then spread half the bacalhau on top of them, and then spread half the onions on top of the bacalhau. Repeat with the second half of each ingredient for a total of six layers. Drizzle the remaining ¼ cup of olive oil over top and bake in a 350° oven for 30 to 40 minutes or until lightly browned on top. Garnish with olives, sliced eggs and chopped parsley.

Serve with lots of freshly ground black pepper.

Serves 6.

Bacalhau Fritters

1 pound bacalhau
2½ cups of stale French bread
⅓ cup olive oil
2 eggs, beaten
¼ cup chopped coriander
¼ cup chopped parsley
1 teaspoon chopped mint leaves
1 tablespoon sweet paprika
   salt and pepper to taste
   oil for frying

Prepare the bacalhau as outlined on page 118. Remove crust from the bread, crumble the white part, and then soak and mash it into the olive oil until the oil is completely absorbed.

In a large bowl combine the beaten eggs, coriander, parsley, mint, paprika, bacalhau, bread mix, salt, and pepper. Beat well. Shape the mix into six flat cakes about 3 inches in diameter.

Heat cooking oil in a skillet and fry the cakes for 3 to 4 minutes on each side. Turn carefully with a spatula. Serve at once.

Serves 6.

Bacalhau with Chick Peas

 1 pound bacalhau
½ cup olive oil
 2 cups thinly sliced onion
 1 14-ounce can of chick peas, drained
 3 large sprigs parsley, chopped
⅓ cup white wine vinegar
 2 cloves garlic, minced
½ teaspoon piri-piri (see page 75) or ¼ teaspoon dried red
   hot pepper flakes
   salt and pepper to taste
 3 hard-boiled eggs, shelled and quartered
10 Calimata olives, pitted and sliced

Prepare bacalhau as outlined on page 118. In a heavy skillet, heat the olive oil and cook the onion slowly until golden. Stir in the bacalhau and heat for 2 minutes.

Then add the chick peas, parsley, vinegar, garlic, piri-piri, salt, and pepper. Cook for 2 more minutes, add the quartered eggs and olives.

Serve hot or room temperature.

Serves 4.

Bacalhau with Eggs

1 pound bacalhau
3 medium-sized potatoes
   vegetable oil for frying
⅓ cup olive oil
1 large onion, peeled and chopped
6 eggs, beaten
   pepper to taste
¼ cup chopped parsley

Prepare the bacalhau as outlined on page 118.

Peel and cut the potatoes into small cubes. Fry potatoes in vegetable oil until golden. Drain on paper towels and set aside.

In a heavy skillet, heat the olive oil and slowly cook the onion until golden. Stir in the bacalhau. Add the eggs to the skillet along with a few generous grinds of black pepper. With a spatula, turn the eggs and fish over medium heat until just set. Fold in the fried potatoes, turn entire contents of the skillet onto a serving platter, sprinkle with parsley, and serve at once.

Serves 4.

Baked Bacalhau with Sausage

1½ pounds bacalhau
⅓ cup olive oil
½ pound chourico, linguica (or Kielbasa) sausage, skinned
    and thinly sliced
1 large ripe tomato cut into ¼ inch slice
    salt and pepper to taste
10 Calimata olives, pitted and sliced

Prepare the bacalhau as outlined on page 118 and leave the bacalhau pieces as big as possible after simmering, skinning, and boning.

Brush a flat ovenproof casserole with some of the olive oil and layer the fish across the bottom. Drizzle the remaining oil over the fish.

Arrange the sliced sausage over the fish, and finally cover the sausage with the tomato slices. Brush tomatoes with a little oil. Sprinkle with salt and pepper to taste. Bake in a 350° oven for 20 minutes, add sliced olives on top and bake 5 or 10 minutes longer.

Serve at once from the baking dish.

Serves 6.

Meat
and Poultry

Liver and Sausage with Fried Potatoes

This is a favorite dish of the region around Lisbon, very quick and easy (see "A Castle by the Sea"). Boil the potatoes and marinate the meats the day before.

½ pound smoked garlic sausage such as chourico, linguica, or keilbasa
1 pound calf liver, sliced thin
½ cup of dry red wine
1 clove garlic, minced
1 teaspoon mixed pickling spices (or cloves, bay leaves, peppercorns)
¼ teaspoon salt

Mix all the above ingredients together, cover, and refrigerate overnight. Then drain off the marinade, strain it, and heat it in a small pot.

4 strips bacon, chopped
1 onion, sliced thin
3 or 4 boiled potatoes, sliced
salt, pepper

In a large frying pan, fry the bacon and add the liver and sausage mixture. Fry until the liver is cooked through. Remove the liver, sausage, and bacon with a slotted spoon and keep warm while you quickly brown the onions and potatoes in the same pan. Add salt and pepper to taste. Serve the meats with the potatoes and onions on a large platter, the hot marinade as a sauce on the side.

Serves 4.

Pork and Clams in a Cataplana

The unusual combination of pork and clams in this classic dish is unique to Portugal. It could be classed as either a soup or a stew, depending on how it is served. In a deep dish with lots of bread on the side, as a soup, was our first experience with it, but on other occasions it was served as a main dish with potatoes or rice . Either way, it is delicious. It gets its name,"Cataplana" from the lidded pot in which it is traditionally cooked (see "An Algarve Lunch").

½ cup olive oil
2 pounds lean pork, cut into one-inch cubes
1 pound linguica or chourico sausage, crumbled or diced
¼ pound prosciutto or cured ham, diced
3 medium onions, chopped
2 tablespoons garlic, minced
3 bay leaves, crumbled
2 teaspoons sweet paprika
1 cup parsley, chopped
2 teaspoons piri-piri (see page 75) or 2 teaspoons red pepper flakes
¾ cup dry white wine
1 can whole tomatoes, broken up
3 dozen fresh clams

In a large skillet with a tight-fitting lid, heat the oil, brown the cubed pork, then the sausage, then the prosciutto. Add the onion and garlic, and brown two minutes more. Then add the bay leaves, paprika, parsley, piri-piri, and the white wine. Cook on high until the wine has lost its alcohol and reduced by half, then add the can of tomatoes with its liquid. Cover and cook on simmer for about 45 minutes or until the pork cubes are tender. (Up to this point this dish can be made as much as a day ahead of time).

Just before serving, place the clams, hinged side down on top of the meat mix, cover tightly, bring to high heat and cook without opening for ten minutes. Discard any clams that do not open.

Serves 6 to 8.

Tripe Oporto Style

If you go to Oporto, Portugal's big seaport to the north, one of the specialties to try is its tripe. Esteemed on the Iberian peninsula, tripe is seldom served here, in the States. It is well worth the effort, though, to prepare this delicious stew. Serve with steamed rice, a simple salad, bread, and a red wine.

1 pound precooked tripe, cut in 1-inch squares
1 meaty veal shank
1 cup dry white beans, soaked overnight
¼ cup olive oil
¼ pound prosciutto or other cured ham, chopped
½ pound chourico sausage, sliced
2 medium onions, chopped
3 large carrots, peeled and sliced
1 clove garlic, minced
½ small chicken cut in 5 or 6 pieces
1 cup chicken broth
½ teaspoon ground cumin
1 teaspoon piri-piri (see page 75) or ½ teaspoon hot red pepper flakes
1 bay leaf
¼ cup chopped parsley
salt and pepper to taste

Drain the soaked beans. Put into a large saucepan, cover with fresh water and simmer for 1½ hours or until tender. Add water as necessary. Set aside.

Place the tripe and veal shank in a large saucepan, cover with water and simmer for 30 minutes or until the tripe is tender. When cool, pick the meat off the veal shank and reserve with the tripe.

Heat olive oil in a large skillet with a lid and sauté the prosciutto, sausage, onions, carrots, garlic, and chicken pieces. Pour in the chicken broth, cumin, piri-piri, bay leaf, parsley, and salt and pepper to taste. Cover and simmer for 20 minutes.

Drain the beans and return them to their large pot. Add the reserved tripe and veal, plus the chicken, sausage, and carrot mix from the skillet. Simmer all for an additional 20 minutes and stir gently several times. There should not be a great deal of liquid, but add more broth or water if needed to prevent burning. The flavors blend if made ahead and reheated.

Check seasonings before serving.

Serves 4.

Chicken (or Rabbit) Braised in Red Wine

This recipe is very similar to the classic French "coq au vin." The Portuguese include much game in their cuisine and are as likely to make this with rabbit as with chicken. You can substitute one for the other, the only difference being that rabbit needs to cook twice as long as chicken (closer to two hours than to one).

¼ cup olive oil
1 2- to 3-pound chicken or rabbit cut into serving pieces
¼ pound minced bacon
1 cup onions, chopped
2 cloves garlic, minced
1 carrot, peeled and sliced
1 bay leaf
½ cup parsley, chopped
1 teaspoon piri-piri (see page 75) or ½ teaspoon hot red pepper flakes
salt and pepper to taste
1 cup dry red wine (or more)
½ cup dry port or ¼ cup brandy
1 tablespoon cornstarch

In a heavy skillet with a lid heat the olive oil and brown the chicken or rabbit pieces. Remove them from the skillet and sauté the bacon, onion, garlic, and carrot in the same oil. Return the meat to the pan and add the bay leaf, parsley, piri-piri, salt and pepper, wine, and port or brandy.

Bring to a boil, reduce to a simmer, cover and cook for 1 hour (chicken) or 2 hours (rabbit). Check the liquid level from time to time and add more wine if necessary. When the meat is tender, remove it to a serving platter.

Mix the cornstarch with ¼ cup of water and slowly add it to the simmering wine sauce, stirring constantly, until it has thickened as much as desired. (It may not be necessary to use all the cornstarch mix.) Simmer one minute more. Pour the thickened sauce over the meat and serve with rice or fried potatoes.

Serves 6.

Braised Leg of Lamb with Sausage

_____

Although pork is by far the favorite meat of the Portuguese, lamb is also commonly served at home and in restaurants. Like pork, it is most often roasted or braised. It is virtually never served pink. This is an attractive and delicious recipe that is typical of Portuguese main dishes.

⅓ cup olive oil
1 boneless leg of lamb, about 3 to 4 pounds, tied
   salt and pepper to taste
1 cup onions, chopped
1 clove garlic, minced
1 pound of chourico sausage, sliced into rings
⅓ pound of prosciutto or other cured ham, diced
1 medium can of whole tomatoes with their liquid
1 bay leaf
½ teaspoon dried thyme
½ cup chopped parsley
½ cup chopped coriander
8 black Calimata olives, pitted and chopped
   additional chopped coriander and parsley
   lemon wedges

In a large deep skillet or Dutch oven with a lid, heat the olive oil. Dry the lamb and sprinkle with salt and pepper. Brown in the oil for several minutes on each side. Remove from the skillet and using the same oil, lightly brown the onion, garlic, sausage rings, and cured ham.

Return the lamb to the skillet. Break up the tomatoes and add them, plus the bay leaf, thyme, parsley, and coriander. Cover, reduce the heat and braise at a slow simmer for 30 minutes per pound or until the lamb is tender—about 2 hours.

Remove the lamb, cut off the strings, and slice into serving portions. Arrange the slices on a serving platter surrounded by the sausage and tomato sauce, and garnished with additional parsley and coriander, chopped olives, and lemon wedges.

Serves 8.

Jeera Meera Masala

Make this recipe with chicken or beef. In Goa and throughout India "masala" means a mixture of spices.

    2 pounds of cubed meat (beef or chicken cut in 1 inch cubes)
    1 inch piece of ginger root, minced
    6 cloves garlic, minced
    2 teaspoon salt
    1 cup water

Combine all ingredients and simmer covered on medium heat until the meat is almost tender. Drain. Save broth.

Masala paste
    1 teaspoon ground cumin powder
    ½ teaspoon ground cinnamon
    ¼ teaspoon ground cloves
    ¼ teaspoon ground cardamom
    ½ teaspoon ground turmeric
    ¼ teaspoon ground pepper
    4 tablespoons vinegar

Mix the above six spices with the vinegar to form a paste. Set aside.

    2 tablespoons vegetable oil
    2 onions, chopped
    2 large potatoes, peeled and cubed

Sauté onions in oil, add the masala paste, and fry for 3 minutes. Do not allow it to burn. Sprinkle with 1 teaspoon of water if it sticks to the pan.

Add the meat and fry for 2 minutes. Add the potatoes, reserved meat broth, and enough water to allow potatoes and meat to cook until tender, about 15 minutes.

Serve with *Fragrant Rice* (see page 101).

Serves 6.

Cozida (Portuguese Boiled Dinner)

The broth of this Portuguese boiled dinner is often served as an excellent soup, while the stew itself is a complete main dish. This version belonged to Rosella Lopes who was born 89 years ago on São Miquel in the Azores and enjoyed a reputation as a fine cook in the Portuguese community of Stonington, Connecticut.

1 bone-in smoked pork shoulder
1 cup dried chick peas—soaked overnight in cold water
1 pound linguica or chourico sausage, crumbled
4 medium potatoes, peeled and cut into large sections
½ cup split peas
1 can of fava beans, drained
½ pound kale, chopped (or cabbage cut in wedges)
1 cup elbow macaroni

In a large pot, cover the pork shoulder with water. Bring to a boil. Skim off the foam as it rises to the surface. Lower the heat and simmer for two hours.

Remove the shoulder from the pot and when it is cool enough to handle, cut off about one pound of meat. Reserve the bone for another use and add the meat to its broth in the pot.

Drain the chick peas. Add them and all other ingredients except the macaroni to the broth. Simmer for several hours more, stirring occasionally and adding more water as necessary.

Add the macaroni for the last 15 minutes. Test for salt and pepper. Add to taste.

Serves 6.

Roast Chicken with Piri-piri

This delicious roast chicken with the piquant skin is best served simply with roast potatoes and perhaps a tomato and mixed greens salad.

2 whole chicken breasts, split
1 tablespoon minced fresh coriander
2 tablespoons piri-piri (see page 75)
⅓ cup fresh lemon juice (1 lemon)

Combine all ingredients and cover chicken with the mixture. Allow to marinate for 2 hours. Roast in a 350° oven for 45 minutes or until done. Baste several times during cooking with the reserved marinade.

Serves 4.

Roast Pork with Piri-Piri

Pork, in its various forms, is by far the most commonly served meat in Portugal. Start this pork loin marinating the day before for the fullest flavor.

1 sweet red bell pepper, seeded and chopped
4 cloves of garlic, chopped
1 teaspoon salt
4 tablespoons of olive oil
3 teaspoons of piri-piri (see page 75) or hot red pepper flakes
   3-pound boneless pork loin, rolled and tied for roasting

Place all the ingredients (except the pork) in a food processor and process until smooth. Rub the meat with the resulting paste and place, covered, in the refrigerator overnight.

The next day preheat the oven to 350°, uncover the meat and place it, as is, in a roasting pan. Roast for about 40 to 45 minutes per pound or until its internal temperature is 185°.

Serves 8.

Roast Pork with Figs

This version of roast pork with its elegant fig sauce serves well as the centerpiece of a formal dinner.

The roast:

    3 small red or green hot peppers or one tablespoon hot red
       pepper flakes
    1 tablespoon salt
    1 tablespoon minced garlic
    4 bay leaves, crumbled
    ⅓ cup olive oil
       3-pound boneless loin of pork, rolled and tied for roasting
    ½ stick butter
    1 cup dry white wine

Remove seeds and mince the hot peppers. In a small bowl, mix together the peppers (or pepper flakes), salt, minced garlic, bay leaves, and olive oil. Place the meat, fat side up, in a roasting pan and rub the marinade over it. Cut the butter into pats and lay along the top of the roast. Pour the wine into the pan. Roast in a pre-heated 350° oven for 1½ hours or until juices run golden clear and the internal temperature registers 170°. Spoon wine and meat juices over the roast every 15 minutes. Add more wine to the pan if needed.

The sauce and garnish:

    3 oranges
    16 moist dried figs
    2 tablespoons brandy

    1 tablespoon honey
    ½ cup orange juice
       salt and pepper to taste

Peel and slice 2 oranges. Remove the stems from 8 figs. Place them with the orange slices, brandy, and honey into a blender or food processor and process until fairly smooth. Set aside.

Remove the stems from the other 8 figs and place them in a small covered saucepan with the orange juice. Simmer for 10 minutes and set aside.

Ten minutes before the roast is done, remove it from the oven. Arrange the whole figs along the top and pour the orange juice over the meat. Return the meat to the oven for 10 minutes to complete its roasting time.

When the meat is finished, carefully cut and remove the strings. Place it on its serving platter and keep warm.

Pour the pan juices into a small saucepan, scraping the pan to include all the flavorful brown bits, and add the puréed orange and fig mix. Bring to a boil and simmer for 5 minutes. Add more white wine if needed. Strain the sauce carefully and add salt and pepper to taste.

Slice the last orange into half round slices to garnish the roast on its platter. Pass the sauce separately.

Serves 8.

Roast Suckling Pig

Roast suckling pig is the meat of celebration in Portugal, often reserved for special occasions. If you can get a small, young pig from the butcher, try this typically Iberian dish (see "Obidos—A Fortified Town"). Serve with fried potatoes and a salad.

½ cup olive oil
1 tablespoon salt
½ teaspoon ground black pepper
2 cloves garlic, mashed
2 tablespoons ground or minced bacon
½ cup chopped parsley
1 cup dry white wine
1 6- or 7-pound suckling pig
(orange sections and additional parsley, reserved for garnish)

Mix all ingredients together and coat the pig in a roasting pan, skin side up. Cover the ears and tail with foil. Roast in a 350° oven for 2½ to 3 hours basting at least 6 times with reserved marinade. Add more white wine if needed. Remove the foil during the last 30 minutes of roasting time.

Serve on a large platter garnished with lots of fresh parsley and orange sections.

Serves 6.

Desserts

Fresh Fruit Compote

The fresh fruits of Portugal are a joy to behold. The village markets are overflowing with luscious oranges from Setúbal, plums from Elvas, strawberries from the Algarve, apricots and peaches from Alcobaça, and large ripe melons and grapes of every description. Choose the ripest fruit of the moment for your compote and be sure to include some bits of dried figs, slivered almonds, crystallized ginger, and a splash of sweet Madeira or port for a typically Portuguese touch.

Pears, peaches, plums, apricots, strawberries, etc.
¼ to ½ cup ruby port or sweet Madeira wine
¼ cup sugar (more or less to taste)
½ cup blanched, slivered almonds
½ cup dried figs, diced or slivered (stems removed)
¼ cup crystallized ginger, minced
Mint leaves for garnish

Wash, pit, peel, and slice fruit as appropriate. Mix the wine and sugar together until the sugar dissolves, then pour over the cut fruit.

Prepare the other ingredients. Add to the fruit in a large bowl. Mix gently, cover and refrigerate for 30 minutes, gently mix once again.

Serve garnished with mint leaves.

Serves 4 to 6.

Orange Custard

Substituting orange juice for the cream in this custard creates a fragrant and light dessert.

2 oranges
6 eggs
1 cup sugar
1 half pint whipping cream
1 tablespoon Grand Marnier (optional)
    orange slices (optional)

Grate the orange rind from the two oranges. Set aside.

Slice the oranges in half and squeeze out all the juice. Combine the rind, juice, eggs, and sugar in a medium sized mixing bowl and beat well until all of the sugar is dissolved.

Generously butter and sprinkle sugar onto the sides and bottom of a 1½ quart ovenproof soufflé dish.

Preheat oven to 350°. Pour mix into the soufflé dish and bake for 40 minutes or until set. Cool and chill.

Whip cream with 1 tablespoon of sugar and Grand Marnier until stiff. Unmold thoroughly chilled custard onto a serving dish.

Garnish with whipped cream and orange slices.

Serves 6.

Sweet Rice Custard

This delicate dessert is lovely after a heavy meal. The Portuguese acquired their taste for rice during their Far East explorations, and today it is cultivated in Portugal, especially in the region around Aveiro.

3 cups of whole milk
½ cup sugar
1 cinnamon stick
outer rind of one lemon
½ cup rice
4 egg yolks
ground cinnamon for garnish

Pour the milk into a heavy-bottomed saucepan. Add the sugar and cinnamon stick. Carefully cut the yellow rind from the lemon in a continuous spiral. Do not cut into the white as it is bitter. Add to the milk. Bring just to a boil and add the rice. Reduce the heat and simmer uncovered for 20 minutes, stirring occasionally. Remove the cinnamon and lemon rind. Allow the milk to cool a little.

Beat the egg yolks lightly and slowly add ¼ cup of the warm milk to them. Now add the yolks to the rest of the milk in the saucepan. Whisk constantly over medium heat until the custard thickens and coats the spoon. Do not allow to boil.

Spoon into 6 individual custard cups and garnish with a sprinkle of ground cinnamon. Chill.

Serves 6.

Pudim Flan

On the Iberian peninsula, flan is a classic dessert and it is difficult to find a restaurant in Spain or Portugal where it is not on the menu. The Portuguese version includes a bit of port wine.

½ cup sugar (for the caramel)
⅓ cup sugar
2 eggs
3 egg yolks
1 cup heavy cream
1 cup milk
1 tablespoon port wine (or brandy)

Place the ½ cup of sugar in a heavy-bottomed small saucepan and heat over low heat for 10 minutes or until the sugar is melted and straw colored. Quickly divide the caramelized sugar between 6 ovenproof custard cups and evenly coat the bottoms. Chill to harden the sugar.

Beat together the rest of the sugar, eggs, egg yolks, cream, milk, and port wine until smooth and the sugar is dissolved. Pour the mix into the custard cups and place them in a roasting pan. Pour enough boiling water into the pan to come halfway up the sides of the cups. Bake for 40 minutes in a 325° oven or until set. Refrigerate until thoroughly chilled.

To unmold, run a knife around the inside edge of each cup and dip the bottoms briefly in very hot water. Invert onto a serving plate.

Garnish with a few berries or a flower.

Serves 6.

Sweet Egg Cakes in Syrup

This extremely delicate egg and syrup confection is often called Angel's Breasts!

1 egg white
5 egg yolks
1 cup sugar
¾ cup water
1 teaspoon lemon juice
1 slice of lemon peel

Preheat the oven to 350°. Generously butter four individual oven-proof custard cups.

Beat the egg white until stiff. Beat the egg yolks until thick and lemon colored. Gently fold in the egg whites and divide the mix into the four cups. Place the cups in an oven pan and pour in enough boiling water to reach halfway up the sides of the cups. Bake for about 10 minutes.

Meanwhile, combine the sugar, water, lemon juice, and lemon peel in a small saucepan. Bring to a boil and continue to boil vigorously for about 4 or 5 minutes or until a medium syrup forms.

When the cakes have cooled a bit, unmold them. Turn each gently in the syrup, place on a serving plate and pour the remaining syrup over the top.

Cover and chill for several hours before serving.

Serves 4.

Ovos Moles

Portuguese desserts tend to be found in one of three broad cate-gories. The first is fresh or preserved fruits, used alone or with soft cheeses. The second includes baked egg and cream custards, and flans (sometimes combined with almonds or port), and the third category utilizes endless combinations of sugar and eggs.

Sugar and egg yolks alone are used to create this rich sauce called "ovos moles." It can be served by itself as a dessert, over fruit, or as an icing for a sponge cake or torte.

⅓ cup water
1¼ cups of sugar
8 egg yolks

In a heavy saucepan over medium heat, dissolve the sugar in the water. Allow to cool. In the meantime, separate the eggs, reserving the whites for another use. With an electric or hand-beater, beat the yolks until they are thick and light yellow. Continuing to beat them, slowly pour in the sugar syrup. Return the egg and sugar mix to the saucepan, and stirring constantly, heat over low heat until thickened enough to coat the spoon.
Do not allow to boil. It will thicken more upon cooling.

Serves 4.

Almond Cake with Ovos Moles

This almond cake, really an almond torte, is delicious when filled and iced with ovos moles (see page 149). Make in advance so the cake can absorb the sauce.

1½ cups blanched almonds
   salt
 6 eggs, separated
¾ cup sugar
 1 teaspoon almond extract

Preheat the oven to 350°. Butter the bottom and sides of a 9-inch round cake pan, cut a round of waxed paper to line the pan, and put additional butter on the paper.

Roast the almonds for 10 minutes and then grind them very fine in a food processor or nut grinder.

Beat the egg whites with a pinch of salt until they hold stiff peaks.

In another bowl, beat the egg yolks and sugar until the mix is thick, pale yellow, and no grains of sugar can be felt. Stir in the almonds and almond extract. Fold the yolks into the whites carefully, pour the batter into the pan and bake for 25 minutes or until the cake feels springy and pulls away from the side of the pan.

Remove from the oven, allow to cool, turn out of the pan and peel off the waxed paper. Carefully split the cooled cake into two layers and spread some ovos moles between and on top of the two layers.

Serves 8.

Sweet Egg Cake with Almonds

A rich almond cake, this dessert uses the familiar ingredients of almonds, eggs and sugar. It is attractive sprinkled with confectioner's sugar and served with fresh berries or sliced peaches.

1 cup roasted almonds, ground
1 cup of sugar
5 eggs, separated
1 tablespoon melted butter

Preheat the oven to 350°. Generously butter and flour 8 individual molds (or one larger mold).

Combine the ground almonds and sugar in a bowl. Beat in the 5 egg yolks one at a time. Continue to beat for several minutes, then add and beat in the butter.

Beat the egg whites until they hold stiff peaks. Gently fold them into the yolk mix. Spoon the mix into the molds and bake for about 20 to 30 minutes or until springy. Allow to cool. Turn out of the molds.

Serves 8.

Almond Cheese Tart

This lovely almond cheese tart combines the dessert ingredients most dear to the Portuguese palette.

The crust:
  ½ cup blanched almonds
  ½ cup unsalted butter, softened
  ¼ cup sugar
  ½ teaspoon vanilla extract
  1 egg
  ¼ teaspoon salt
  2 cups all-purpose flour

On a cookie sheet, roast the almonds in a 350° oven for 8 minutes. Grind them fine in a food processor.

In a deep mixing bowl, cream the butter and sugar with an electric mixer until fluffy. Add the vanilla, egg, salt, and almonds. Continue to beat well for 2 minutes. Add the flour by hand and mix until just incorporated. Gather dough into a ball, wrap and chill for one hour while you make the filling.

When thoroughly chilled, roll out the pastry on a floured board or between pieces of waxed paper. Fit it into a 9-inch pie pan and crimp the edge decoratively. Bake for 10 minutes in a 350° oven. Cool.

The filling:
  ½ cup cream cheese, softened
  1½ cups of unsalted pot or farmer cheese

¾ cup sugar
 2 eggs and 1 egg yolk
½ teaspoon ground cinnamon
½ teaspoon salt
⅓ cup whole blanched almonds

In a deep mixing bowl, beat the cream cheese, pot cheese, sugar, eggs (including egg yolk), cinnamon, and salt with an electric mixer until smooth. Pour mix into the baked pie shell and place in a pre-heated 350° oven for 20 minutes. Remove from the oven and arrange the blanched almonds in an attractive pattern on top. Return to the oven for 10 additional minutes or until set. Cool before slicing.

Serves 6.

Lethri

Esther reminded us that the combination of coconut from India with the bread and almonds from Portugal makes this typically Goan dessert a true hybrid (see "A Remnant of the Age of Exploration").

3 cups sugar
2 cups water
28 ounces of dried, sweetened, flaked coconut
1 loaf of firm white bread
¾ pound raisins
3 ounce butter
½ teaspoon vanilla extract
½ pound of blanched slivered almonds

In a heavy deep saucepan, cook the sugar, water, and coconut together for 5 minutes.

Trim all crust from bread and shred it. Add to the coconut mix. Add the raisins. Cook gently, stirring constantly until the mix dries a little. Stir in the butter and vanilla. Pour into many small custard cups or cupcake forms to set.

Garnish with the slivered almonds.

Quince Preserves

The quince is a native of southeast Asia and was brought by the Muslims to Portugal. This "marmelada" is served with mild fresh cheeses after a meal—instead of on bread for breakfast—and is famous throughout Portugal.

   1 pound quince, peeled and cored
   2 cups water
1½ cups sugar
     all of the peel (not the white) of 1 lemon
⅛ teaspoon cinnamon

Slice the cleaned quince, cover with water in a large sauce pan and boil until tender. Drain and purée in a blender or food processor.

Boil the 2 cups of water, sugar, lemon peel, and cinnamon. Add the quince purée and simmer until thick. Remove from the heat and take out the lemon peel. This preserve can be refrigerated, frozen or sealed in sterile jars.

Makes 2 cups.

Figs Filled with Almonds and Chocolate

Beautiful almond trees bloom each spring in the south, and the almond figures heavily in the pastries and sweets of Portugal. One of the simplest confections is the following after dinner treat.

¾ cup blanched almonds
½ cup chocolate chips, chopped, or ½ cup grated semi-sweet
    chocolate
¼ cup sugar
10 to 12 dried figs

Toast the almonds on a cookie sheet in a 350° oven for 8 minutes. Grind them in a food processor. Mix the ground almonds, sugar, and chocolate together.

Cut off the hard stem of the figs and make a cut with a sharp knife to open them. Pack one teaspoon of the mix into each fig and close. Place in the still hot oven for seven minutes.

Serve with Port wine.

Serves 4.

Almond and Fig Bonbons

The figs and almonds grown in the southern Algarve region of Portugal are delicious and find their way to markets in all parts of the country. Paired, they are sublime. You will need a food processor for this recipe.

1 cup whole almonds
1 pound dried figs
¼ teaspoon ground cinnamon
1 tablespoon brandy
½ cup of granulated sugar

Spread almonds in a single layer on a cookie sheet and toast them in a 350° oven for about 8 or 9 minutes.

Remove and discard the stems from the figs. Place all ingredients except the sugar into the container of a food processor and process until smooth. Divide and roll mix lightly into 1-inch balls.

Put sugar in a shallow bowl. Coat each ball in turn with the sugar and arrange on a doily on your prettiest dish.

Serve after dinner with a glass of port or Madeira.

Serves 6.

A Word About Wines

Portugal has been a land of vineyards for well over 2,000 years. The Phoenicians and later the Greeks and Romans have all cultivated grapes for wine. Although after the fall of Rome, during the era of the barbarian invasions, and later under the Muslim domination, wine production dropped, for the past 500 years there has been a steady growth in acres under cultivation. Indeed, wine exporting today forms an important part of Portugal's international revenues.

In recent years, especially, the government has helped to encourage and regulate designated wine producing regions. There are now ten officially recognized areas, each producing distinctly different products. Some are world renown, some seldom found beyond Portugal's shores. If you have an interest in the cuisine of Portugal, a working knowledge of her wines, and their appropriate place in menu planning, is essential.

Most of the important wines and ports are grown in the northern quarter of the country along her border there with Spain and in the valley of the Douro river, but there are also important areas along the Mondego river, in and around Lisbon, and in the far southern Algarve region. The volcanic island of Madeira, uninhabited until the 15th century, now produces the world famous fortified wines of the same name.

There are hundreds of small vineyards of limited production that only supply table wines to local establishments; and in the case of Buçaco, to just one hotel. To taste those wines you will have to journey to their source. However, increasing amounts of non-fortified wines are finding their way to shops outside Portugal. Today it is possible to obtain Portugal's whites, reds, and rosés all over the world.

The most well-known, though, are the fortified wines—the ports and Madeiras. They are seldom drunk with a meal, but rather as aperitifs or as dessert and after dinner drinks. Of the ports, by law all will say "Oporto" on the label and be sealed with a government tag. The grapes for these great wines are grown in the steep Douro river valley, and the fermented juice is transported for aging and export to Oporto, Portugal's second largest city, 150 miles downstream on the Atlantic coast. While Vintage ports are very expensive, having aged and matured many years in their bottles, there are several other pleasing varieties to consider.

White port is very dry and should be served chilled as an aperitif before a Portuguese meal. Ruby port is dark and semi-sweet, usually served in cooler weather for sipping after dinner. Tawny ports are aged in wood casks for at least five years and take on their lovely color from the wood. Aged Tawny ports, some up to 40 years old, are very elegant, and finally, the Vintage ports are at the top of the quality line. All but the White ports should be served with quality cheeses, fruits, sweets and nuts, or alone.

The island of Madeira, off the coast of Africa, has been planted in vineyards for hundreds of years and produces a brandy-fortified wine that was even more famous two hundred years ago than it is today. It, like port, is produced in a very dry version called Sercial, usually drunk as an aperitif, and Boal and Malmsey, which are sweet and heavy and served with or after dessert. The production of both ports and Madeiras have had a close association with the British for three hundred years, and their trade partnership is to this day of real importance. As with names on the sherries of Spain, the names of the greatest producers of ports and

Madeiras are very often English.

Besides the island of Madeira and the port region of the Douro valley, the government has officially named eight other regions. In the far north lies the biggest region, called Vinho Verde. These wines are often exported and are familiar to consumers outside Portugal. The reds are seldom exported, and it is the light, fruity, young, slightly sparkling whites that are found most often. They are appropriate to serve with any fish dish, with the exception of bacalhau (which always takes a red).

The second largest region is the Dão, in and around the Dão and Mondego rivers in north central Portugal. The reds of this region are quite well known. They have a strong mature quality and lovely rich brown-red color. Serve these with any of the pork or lamb roasts, or any other robust meat dishes in this book. Nearby, closer to the Atlantic coast, is the Bairrada wine region with its reds. These are also a good choice with game and roasts. Not many whites are produced in these two areas, and virtually none are exported.

Four designated regions cluster around Lisbon on the Atlantic coast. Colares, in the extreme west, grows its grapevines in the sandy coastal soil and produces some of the best reds in Portugal. They are slow to mature and very dark in color. Try them with roast suckling pig, rabbit, or other game. Close by is Bucelas, known for its white wines, with their subtle color and slightly astringent taste. If you can find these, they are a good choice to serve with fish and white meats such as chicken and veal. Cara-cavelos, nearest to Lisbon, produces a fortified sweet dessert wine that, if it can be found, is worth a try. Across the Tagus river lies the Setúbal region that produces an unusual honey-flavored fortified dessert wine called Moscatel, as well as some fine reds. The well-known Lancers rosé also comes from this region.

The last region, the Algarve, along the southern coast, produces mostly red wines. Few are exported, and most are used within the area. They are fairly inexpensive, and the thousands of tourists there enjoy these good table wines.

The market for Portuguese wines increases each year, and greater variety than ever is available in better wine shops. Be on the lookout for them. They are usually identified by region or town within the region and are the perfect accompaniment to a savory Portuguese meal.

Index

Portuguese and Indian words in *italics*. Recipe headings in SMALL CAP LETTERS